Other Books by Mr. Virgines:
Saga of the Colt Six-Shooter
Famous Guns and Gunners

WESTERN LEGENDS AND LORE

WESTERN LEGENDS AND LORE

by
George E. Virgines

Published by
Leather Stocking Books
Pine Mountain Press, Inc. Publishing Group
P.O. Box 13604
Wauwatosa, WI 53226

Editor: Marilyn A. Brilliant
Cover Illustration: Ernest Lisle Reedstrom
Typesetting and Production Art: Trade Press Typographers

ISBN: 0-89769-052-4 PAP

*It is my pleasure to dedicate this book
to my wife and pardner, Loraine.*

CONTENTS

 1. Pawnee Bill — The Legend 1
 2. William S. Hart — A Western Movie Legend..... 13
 3. Gun Lore of The Old West 25
 4. Canvas Lawmen 41
 5. Presenting Legend Maker: Stan Lynde 57
 6. Badges and Badge Toters...................... 71
 7. Mementoes of The 101 Wild West Show 85
 8. Legendary Poster Cowboys 99
 9. The Lore of The Bull Whip................... 111
10. Wagon Wheels Keep Rollin'................... 119
11. Horse-Shoe Lore 133
12. Tell Tale Marks 145
13. Birth of a Colt Commemorative Legend......... 157
14. The Last Legend 1873 - 1981 167

Introduction

Much of our Western heritage and history is contained in our legends that exemplifies the frontier, west-ward-ho era.

The fabulous feats and figures that contributed to the legends are many, even in contemporary times. They came from all walks of life including farmers, ranchers, storekeepers, miners, scouts, cowboys, Indians, soldiers, gamblers, ladies of the "Red Light" district; gunfighters from both sides of the law. Added to this are the many writers, artists, and even the Western movie heroes. The list could go on, and on, and all of their contributions have been duly recorded.

The tools of their trade, such as equipment, accroutements, and the way they used them became the lore that has added to our education.

The legends are preserved by word of mouth, books, newspapers, records, pictures, and paintings. From the lore came the many relics, antiques, etc. Today they are popularly known as the collectables that have formed a link between the past and present.

It has been this author's efforts and wish to weld these facts that form Western Legends and Lore.

George E. Virgines
Author

CHAPTER I

"PAWNEE BILL, THE LEGEND"

The frontier of the old West has spawned many famous characters and such individuals who had the nick-name "Bill" included as part of their surname have seemed to left their mark in frontier history. To name a few are especially "Wild Bill" Hickok, "Buffalo Bill" Cody, and "Pawnee Bill" Lillie.

Pawnee Bill was actually Major Gordon W. Lillie. He became more popular as Pawnee Bill in connection with his famous Wild West Show. In later years his association with Buffalo Bill made his name synonymous with Western style entertainment. This was most apparent when the two "Bills" combined their two great shows with the imposing title of "Buffalo Bill's Wild West and Pawnee Bill's Great Far East Combined" in 1908.

Major Lillie's involvement with wild west shows was the most spectacular and glamorous part of his personality. He was also a leader of the Oklahoma Boomers in the land rush of the early 1880's and again in 1893. Pawnee Bill may have been physically small in stature but he was a giant in the building of the old West and the Oklahoma Territory.

Gordon W. Lillie was born in Bloomington, Illinois on February 14, 1860 and as a youth, with his family joined a covered wagon train bound for Kansas. The main tools for a pioneer family to settle in a wild and virgin territory was a good team of horses, a plow, axe, and quite naturally a gun. It was just as important to have a gun and know how to use it as any tool on the frontier. So young Gordon soon developed the skills as a hunter to supply meat for the family. This new skill would become most advantageous in later years when he became a buffalo hunter and in the future, as a sharp shooter in his own wild west show.

In his early years he first became a teacher in an Indian school on the Pawnee Indian Reservation. This soon led into a lasting friendship of the entire tribe as he also learned their language and customs. Pawnee Bill's great understanding of the Indians was instrumental in his becoming a government interpreter in all dealings between the federal agencies and the Indian tribe. In later years he was bestowed the highest honor given by the Pawnees to a white man, "White Chief of the Pawnees."

Similar to young men before him and after, Lillie was inspired by the tales of the wild and exciting frontier and wouldn't be satisfied until he ventured further west to see this amazing new country. He outfitted himself with the traditional cowboy clothes, horse, saddle, and the main tools of the trade for a cowboy, revolver and rifle.

Gordon Lillie learned the way of the frontier with the Indians, and later with association and pardner of an Indian trader named "Trapper Tim" McCain. With him he trapped and hunted buffalo using the old .50 caliber Springfield breech-loading needle gun so popular on the plains. Later the Henry repeating rifle became one of his favorite weapons.

Buffalo Bill Cody had always been Gordon's hero ever

since he saw him once and became so fascinated that he read and followed Cody's exploits at every opportunity. In 1883 when Lillie was offered the chance to be in charge of a band of Pawnee Indians with Buffalo Bill's Wild West Show, it was an offer and a childhood dream, that he could not refuse. It was a great experience for Gordon being with Buffalo Bill's show and it was during this period that he met his future wife, May Manning, who was destined to become a famous "Champion Woman Horseback Rifle and Revolver Shot."

In 1888 Pawnee Bill was at last to have his own Wild West Show, it appeared to be a huge success. He not only had his wife May as a star attraction but also the famed Annie Oakley who had left Buffalo Bill's show. But in spite of all this the show lost money — bad weather, competition from Buffalo Bill, and unpaid debts all contributed to the downfall of his first efforts as a showman.

Eventually Pawnee Bill went back West to Wichita, Kansas, where he became involved with the Boomer movement. He was always an admirer of Captain D. L. Payne who was constantly campaigning to open the Oklahoma Indian Territory for homesteading. Upon the death of Capt. Payne, Lillie became more active in Boomer groups. In 1889 he was on hand to lead his band of Boomers in the opening of the Cherokee Strip in Oklahoma.

Displayed in the noted Saunders Gun Museum of Berryville, Arkansas there is featured a Colt Single Action Army revolver, caliber .45, black powder model, that Pawnee Bill presented to Buck Saunders on February 2, 1936 and is alleged to have been carried and fired by Pawnee Bill on that eventful day of the Oklahoma land rush.

After the great Oklahoma land run Pawnee Bill was to discover that he had become famous as his name was mentioned in many of the newspaper accounts of this historical era in which he participated as a leader. He became a national figure known as "Pawnee Bill."

He now more than ever wanted to get back to his first love and hit the circus trail. The Major organized his new show which was entitled "Pawnee Bill's Historical Wild West, Indian Museum and Encampment." The show was described as "America's National Western Entertainment" headed by the now famous Pawnee Bill and featuring his equally famous wife, May Lillie, "Champion Girl Shot of the West." It was a star studded show that traveled from the Atlantic to the Pacific and from Mexico to Canada. In 1894 he took the show to Europe in which it became a huge success.

During his life time Major Lillie was to have many guns accredited to his collection, and even afterward, that collectors have to beware of fakes. The earliest guns to be acclaimed as Pawnee Bill guns were advertised in a guns catalog in 1955 put out by a Hy Hunter, and once again several years ago in 1975 by an arms dealer in a gun collector's type magazine. The guns in question were very elegant and unique being gold plated, ivory handled, with 5½ inch barrel lengths, serial numbers 14844 and 14855. They were English proofed, caliber .450 Boxer. The backstraps of the guns were engraved in script, "Major Gordon W. Lillie." This is the only thing that gives these guns association to Pawnee Bill, as of now. Just exactly when these alleged guns were in Pawnee Bill's possession is unknown. According to the serial numbers range these Colts Single Action Army revolvers would be dated as manufactured in 1874 or 1875. One other item of interest is that Pawnee Bill never obtained the title of Major until later years.

Pawnee Bill's great Wild West Show grew bigger and more popular, and in spite of competition he did a tremendous business.

That he favored Colt single actions is authenticated by Colt factory records, and in turn Colt also favored Pawnee Bill enough to present him with several pairs of Single Action Colts. It is known that Pawnee Bill often visited the Colt Company.

The Colt Company was kind enough to supply this author with a list of Colt Single Action Army revolvers recorded in their records as either being bought or presented to Pawnee Bill over the period of years in his life time.

On April 30, 1891 he ordered two Colt Single Actions, Serial Nos. 140472 and 140502 in caliber .44 Smoothbore with 5½ inch barrel lengths, and they were shipped directly to

The famous "Bill's" of show business. Left Pawnee Bill and right, Buffalo Bill.

A poster advertising the famous Pawnee Bill show.

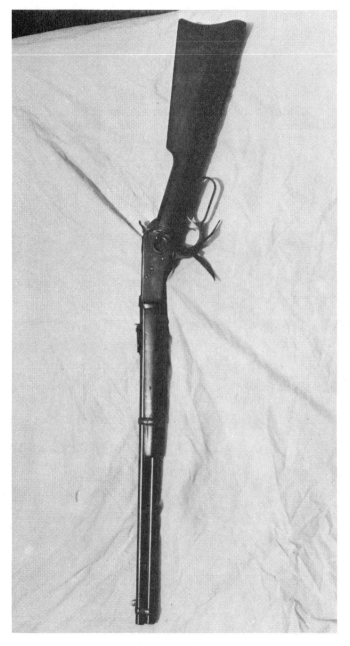

Pawnee Bill's saddle-ring carbine Winchester M1892, caliber .44-40 smoothbore, Serial No. 378879.

Pawnee Bill's Colt Frontier six-shooter, cal. 44-40 smoothbore, Serial No. 140472, 5½-inch barrel and eagle grips. *Graham Burnside*

him. Of these two unique smoothbore Colts only one has yet come to light, and that is serial number 140472 and is well preserved in a private collection.

These smoothbore Colts fired shot, instead of a bullet, to "improve" and/or demonstrate the shooters accuracy in shooting exhibitions. Plus, it was a great deal safer. The use of shot was a safety precaution were spectator's safety was naturally of prime importance. Even though a shot-shell would scatter there still remained a certain amount of skill involved to hit the glass ball targets used when thrown in the air. The smoothbores were all slightly choked similar to a shotgun bore, however the exterior appearance of a smoothbore handgun or rifle shows no indication of the unique caliber.

Also shipped on the same date were another pair of Colt Single Actions, Serial Numbers 133172 and 135785 with conventional 5½ inch barrels in caliber .44-40, these were nickel plated and had pearl grips.

In 1902 the Colt Company presented to Pawnee Bill a pair of Single Action Army Colts with 7½ inch barrels, caliber .45, blued, and also with pearl grips. They had Serial Numbers 229592 and 226214 and were shipped on July 19, 1902 and inscribed — "Presented to Pawnee Bill From The Colt Co."

Once again on June 9, 1906 Major Lillie received from the Colt factory a pair of Colt Sikngle Action Army revolvers, Serial Numbers 275643 and 278226, in caliber .45, 4¾ inch barrels, nickel plated, gilt cylinders and engraved possibly by Cuno A. Helfricht, a master engraver for Colt Company for many years, or his shop, on the backstrap were inscribed — Presented to Pawnee Bill by The Colt P.T.A. Mfg. Co." The above two pairs of historic Pawnee Bill Colts, listed in the Colt records are also mentioned in the excellent and scholarly publication "The Book of Colt Engraving" by R. L. Wilson, well known author and expert on Colt firearms. The whereabouts of these Colts is unknown at this time.

Pawnee Bill is also listed in the Colt's records as purchasing their first large heavy frame, double action revolver, the Colt M1878 Model. The book popularly known as the Colt "bible" is "The Book of Colt Firearms" by R. Q.

Sutherland and R. L. Wilson also mentions this fact.

This man of many guns, Major Lillie was just not partial to handguns. He also is a rifleman. Displayed for many years in the famous (now defunct), Andy Palmer's Inn and Great Guns of Dearborn, Michigan, a Marlin Model 36, Lever Action rifle, caliber .44-40 which is according to a plaque having been presented to the famous sharp-shooter gal, Annie Oakley by Pawnee Bill. Inscribed on the stock is the story that the Major had the gun smoothbored, but when Annie found out she did not use the gun as it was against her principles to cheat the public. Many years ago the Andy Palmer gun collection was sold and auctioned off so it is unknown at this time what happened to this rifle.

In 1908 the two "Bills", Pawnee Bill and Buffalo Bill combined their two shows to become one of the greatest entertainment attractions to tour the country. The combined shows were a huge success and lasted until 1913 at which time Buffalo Bill went with the Sells Floto Show.

A most interesting story concerning two Winchester rifles related to Pawnee Bill was uncovered just a couple of years ago. One rifle, a Winchester M1892 Saddle Ring Carbine, Serial No. 378879, caliber .44-40 Smoothbore, 20 inch barrel, and a nickel plated butt plate, the balance of the gun blued, was discovered at a gun show in Houston, Texas. Naturally this gun being of a smoothbore inspired a follow-up in his history as most smoothbore guns have a wild west show flavor. In checking with the Winchester Gun Museum records it was discovered that this rifle and another, same type, caliber, and smoothbore with Serial No. 368511 were returned to the Winchester factory to be reworked. Number 378879 was shipped originally on April 8, 1907 and Number 368511 was shipped March 14, 1907, and both reworked March 28, 1917 on the same work order and shipped back to the owner. Unfortunately Winchester records do not list the buyers or customers. But both rifles being of smoothbore caliber definitely would be of the type for most commonly used in wild west shows and certainly would receive a lot of additional use and abuse.

Circumstances that eventually associated these two rifles

to Pawnee Bill were the research and letters from the records of the University of Oklahoma, Norman, Oklahoma, that Major Gordon W. (Pawnee Bill) Lillie presented Winchester M1892, Serial Number 368511 (the companion rifle to Serial Number 378879) to Walter Ferguson, famed newspaper publisher of Oklahoma, also a noted gun collector. The exact presentation date is unknown but had to take place after March 1917. In tracing the other Winchester, it had traded hands several times until it was found in Houston. It is now in a private collection.

Major Lillie finally retired to his beautiful home and ranch on top of Blue Hawk Peak in Pawnee, Oklahoma. He had named the place Blue Hawk after his Pawnee Indian friend. The $100.000 mansion is a show place and now open to the public as a State Park and Museum. The house stands furnished as it was on completion in 1910. It is as picturesque as Pawnee Bill. Everything is special — the exterior and interior with all of its imported paneling, flooring, chandeliers, fireplaces, and decorations. The entrance has a massive stone gateway with the words "Buffalo Ranch" in metal letters over the arch, and steel initials "P.B." made from the barrel of a rifle once carried by his friend Major Frank North.

In 1930 the Major built "Pawnee Bill's Old Town and Indian Trading Post" at his ranch. Here he put on shows and displays, but unfortunately it burned down in 1939 and never was rebuilt.

On August 31, 1936 the Major and his wife, May, went to Taos, New Mexico to celebrate their Golden Anniversary and repeat their wedding vows. Two weeks later they were involved in an automobile accident in Oklahoma and May Lillie died four days later from the results of injuries received in the accident. Pawnee Bill receovered, but life wasn't the same for him without May. Six years later on February 3, 1942, he died, just eleven days before his 82nd birthday.

With the passing away of Major Gordon W. Lillie it was also the end of an era and the end of a great Westerner.

BIBLIOGRAPHY

Ron Wagner, Historian, Colt Firearms Division, Hartford, CT.

T. E. Hall, Curator, Winchester Museum of Firearms, New Haven, CT.

"Pawnee Bill" *By Glen Shirley.*

"Lives & Legends of Buffalo Bill" *By Don Russell.*

"The Book of Colt Firearms: *By R. Q. Sutherland & R. L. Wilson.*

"The Book Of Colt Engraving" *By R. L. Wilson.*

"Saga of The Colt Six-Shooter" *By George E. Virgines.*

"A Study of the Colt Single Action Army Revolver" *By Kopec, Graham & Moore.*

"The Winchester Book: *By Geo. Madis*

Saunders Gun Museum, Berryville, Arkansas.

University of Oklahoma Library, Norman, Okla.

Oklahoma Historical Society, Okla. City., Okla.

Pawnee Bill Museum, Pawnee, Okla.

Souvenir Program of Buffalo Ranch and Its Owner Pawnee Bill — 1911.

Program — Buffalo Bill Wild West & Pawnee Bill Great Far East — 1909.

CHAPTER II

WILLIAM S. MART —
A WESTERN MOVIE LEGEND

If ever there was a man who was the prototype and contributed to the legends and ideas of the Western hero, that man had to be William S. Hart. One of the first western movie stars to gain nation-wide popularity, his career started in 1914 and he retired in 1925 during which period he made over one hundred pictures.

Hart was more than just an actor, for he had written and produced many movies. He authored a number of books and articles, and animals and especially horses were one of his first loves. He was a collector of western Americana such as Indian artifacts, fine original paintings and bronzes of such famous artists as Russell, Remington, Flagg, Beil, Cristadora and others.

In all of his movies, Hart portrayed the steely-eyed, fast-drawing, sharp-shooting gunslinger. He took great pride in his dexterity with guns.

William S. Hart was born in Newburgh, New York in 1874 and later moved to Illinois, Iowa, Wisconsin, Minnesota, and on westward. As a boy, he grew up among the Sioux Indians, cowmen and ranch hands. Spending his early years in the Dakota prairies, he learned to ride and shoot. His love for the color and excitement of the early west contributed toward the authenticity and authority that he portrayed in his pictures.

Hart had a great inclination toward the stage and, in his early years, he headed east and on to Europe to study acting. During this period he struggled doing many odd jobs as iceman, clerk, and other part time employment.

He became a successful Shakespearean actor and starred in many successful stage plays. It wasn't until the age of 40, with an established stage reputation, that he began his motion picture career. It was in this medium that he really gained fame. His experiences as a trail-herd cowboy and knowledge of the early west offered striking realism to his pictures. In Hart's own words, "The truth of the west meant more to me than a job and always will."

Hart starred in his first western movie in 1914; in fact, he played the villain. But this was to change in subsequent pictures. Many of Hart's earlier films were shot on the 101 Ranch of Marland, Oklahoma. James Ince, director of Hart's films leased the entire 101 Ranch Wild West Show, so Hart used much of the ranch equipment and many riders.

Because of his great fondness for his horse, Bill Hart was perhaps one of the first western stars to set the example of giving his horse top billing. His favorite horse, a pinto, named Fritz, was starred in a movie titled, "Pinto Ben." This same horse was ridden by Hart in most of his movies.

In fact Bill rode Fritz from 1914 to 1926, he titled his pinto horse "The Greatest All-Around Horse That Ever Lived." He taught him how to pose, kneel, play dead, and other tricks. Fritz is buried on the Hart Ranch along with many other of Bill's pet animals.

As Bill Hart's fame grew, so did his circle of friends. Wyatt Earp was a close friend and the two men corresponded for many years. There are about two dozen of Earp's letters on file at the Hart ranch that these famous characters exchanged. Wyatt Earp being such a close friend to Bill Hart wrote of his feelings about politics and even his anger over the many untruths he felt were printed about his colorful life. Even Mrs. Wyatt Earp wrote to Bill to thank him for his expressed concern to a newspaper story that had written unkindly about Earp. In one of Earp's letters he sent Hart a quirt that had been made by a woman in the Yuma, Arizona, prison. Earp once wrote a script which he hoped that Hart would star in and Hart was a pallbearer at Wyatt Earp's funeral.

Another great of the western frontier was Bat Masterson. Theirs was a mutual admiration by both men. In later years, Masterson, then a sports writer for a New York newspaper, said, "William S. Hart is a true type of that reckless nomad who flourished on the border when the sixshooter was the final arbiter of all disputes between man and man . . ."

Other famed characters that Hart enjoyed a friendship with were Charles Siringo, famous range detective; Bill Tilghman, frontier lawman, Will Rogers, the Miller Brothers of the 101 Ranch and more notables.

One of Hart's western heroes was Wild Bill Hickok whom he portrayed in one of his movies. In fact, his portrayal was so realistic that he had to give a private exhibition, timed by a stop watch, to convince some Los Angeles newspapermen that he could really do some of the fast and fancy two-gun shooting, Hickok style.

Bill Hart's last movie, titled, "Tumbleweeds" was one of his best. In 1939, the film was re-issued with Hart giving an eight-minute prologue that was both impressive and unforgettable.

In 1926 he retired to his Horseshoe Ranch located in Newhall, California. He lived there until his death on June 23, 1946 at the age of 72.

Those who have never had the privilege of seeing this famed old western star can visit the William S. Hart Park which contains 243 acres of rolling hills above Newhall.

Hart stipulated in his will that his home and ranch be donated to the county as a public park, his home as a museum. Here at Horseshoe Ranch, which contain Hart's home, "La Loma de Los Vientos," are exhibit relics of Hart's career and of western Americana. The rooms have all of the original furnishing, Indian attire, historical objects, and many of his personal mementos and valuable records of Hart's life and friends.

One item of interest is that a number of personal items scattered throughout the ranch are marked with Hart's own registered cattle brand "WSH." This was used as his monogram and ownership mark.

Included are eighteen paintings and five bronze statues by Charles M. Russell. Other famous artists represented in the art-work collection are C. C. Crestadora, Federic Remington, Joe D. Young, James Montgomery Flagg, A. P. Proctor and Clarence Ellsworth.

Included amongst Hart's personal collection are the many books he wrote most of which are now out of print and considered as collector's items. To name a few are "Pinto Ben & Other Stories" inspired by his horse Fritz. A series entitled "The Golden West Boys" and Bill's own story "My Life, East and West." Charley Russell painted the cover jacket depicting Bill on his favorite pinto horse, Fritz.

Included in the interesting display of relics is the personal collection of firearms of Bill Hart. The more historic pieces include a Colt Single Action Army revolver, serial No. 70361, caliber .44-40, with 4¾-inch barrel, and engraved "Bill" on the back of the grips. This particular gun is alleged once to have belonged to the notorious gunman, Bill The Kid. Hart is supposed to have paid a fabulous price for this particular shootin' iron.

In later years added prestige was given to this gun, when Bill Hart coached Robert Taylor and Johnny Mack Brown in their respective versions of "Billy The Kid" movies. Hart thought that the donated use of the Billy The Kid gun gave their portrayals more authenticity.

Another impressive Colt Single Action with serial No.

A part of Bill Hart's gun collection. Guns Nos. 2 and 3 used by Hart in many of his movies. Gun No. 4 is supposed to have once belonged to Billy the Kid. It is a Colt SAA, Serial No. 70361. Gun No. 1 is a Colt cap and ball conversion 1849 model.

Los Angeles County Museum

17

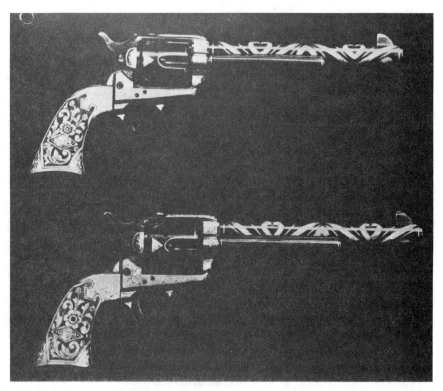

A pair of fancy engraved Colt single action Army revolvers with 7½ inch barrels, caliber .45, Serial No. 346014 and 342963. William S. Hart had these fine guns engraved for his son. *Connecticut State Library*

Bill Hart's favorite horse, "Fritz," with riding gear.

Wm. V. Morrison

Bill Hart's distinguished Stetson hat and leather cuffs.   *Wm. S. Hart Museum*

A favorite fighting pose of two-gun William S. Hart.

26894, caliber .45 and with "NRT" carved in the right grip, was presented to Bill Hart by the citizens of Dodge City, Kansas in 1917. This gun had belonged to Sheriff Chalk Beeson, who had taken it from the body of the last bad man killed on Front Street.

Al Jennings, self-styled outlaw, gave one of his guns to Hart. This particular piece was a Colt Single Action, single No. 32157, caliber .45, with the initials "AJ" carved in the right wood grip.

Bill Hart's favorite guns, used in many rip-roaring movies, were a Colt Single Action Army revolver, serial No. 249742, caliber .45, 5½ inch barrel, with stag grips and a Colt New Service double action revolver, also .45 caliber, serial No. 307955, with stag grips.

One foreign handgun was presented to Hart by General Robert L. Eichelberger. This is a Japanese Nambu, caliber 9 MM revolver, serial No. 26771. The general had taken this gun from a prisoner during the Philippine campaign during the Second World War.

Perhaps the most important and sentimental firearm in Hart's collection was a Marlin lever action rifle, caliber .38/55, Model 1881, serial No. 151116. It was given to Hart by his father, who had taken it away from an outlaw.

Like any proud father, Bill Hart couldn't wait for his son to grow up. When his son, Bill, Junior, was only two years old at Christmas time, he gave him a beautiful hand-tooled saddle trimmed in silver and a pair of fine engraved Colt Single Actions. It took two months for the skilled craftsman to completely engrave this pair of Colts with elaborate inlaid silver and gold with the design of hearts down the barrel. The silver grips bear the initials "WSH." Both guns are .45 caliber, with 7½ inch barrels, and serial nos. 346014 and 342963. The only evidence of these ornate Colts is a photograph and letter Hart sent to the Colt Company in January, 1925. The letter is as follows:

Gentlemen:
I am enclosing photos of two guns of your make that I had inlaid

and presented to my son, William S. Hart, Jr., age two years and four months. When the little fellow has grown to manhood and his Dad has crossed the Big Divide, he will be a two-gun Bill — just as his Dad was.

When I was a boy on the Frontier, I saw many guns that had been inlaid by some of those who liked fancy shootin' irons, but I never saw anything as handsome as the guns now owned by my son.

When the case is first opened their brilliancy is such one would think them studded with diamonds.

It gives me pleasure to send these photos to you. The old single action Colt .45 is my favorite.

Very sincerely yours,
William S. Hart

It would be interesting to know what happened to these guns, as they are not displayed at the William S. Hart Museum.

One other gun that is supposed to be related to Bill Hart is displayed in the famous Harold's Club Gun Collection in Reno, Nevada. This historic piece is a Colt Single Action, .44 caliber, with a 4¾ inch barrel, serial No. 65888. It is an old worn black powder model and carved on the left grip is "Cimarron 1889" and on the right grip, "W. S. Hart" with a heart around the initials.

William S. Hart is long gone, but his legendary memories are contained in the many historic mementoes at his ranch home. Here he is on canvas executed by the famous Western artist and friend, Charles M. Russell, and also in bronze in the pose so well associated with Hart as the Two-Gun Man by Cristadora. This unique item was noted in an art gallery, in Scottsdale, Arizona, several years ago. It was very impressive weighing 130 pounds and being two feet tall. The many movies that Hart made are testimonial of his strive for realism in the portrayal of the real old west.

BIBLIOGRAPHY

"My Life East and West" *By Wm. S. Hart.*

"The Hall of Fame of Western Film Stars" *By Ernest N. Coreau.*

"A Pictorial History of The Western Film: *By Wm. K. Everson.*

"The Westerner" *By Geo. N. Fenin & Wm. K. Everson.*

"Saga of The Colt Six-Shooter" *By George E. Virgines.*

Colt Firearms Division, Hartford, CT.

Harold's Club, Reno, Nevada.

True West — May-June 1968 "Wyatt Earp's Letters".

"101 Ranch" *By Collings & England.*

Lloyd P. Hiatt, Supervisor, Wm. S. Hart County Park & Museum, Newhall, CA.

The Western Horseman — Apr. 1973 — "Wm. S. Hart and Fritz".

Connecticut State Library, Colt Collection, Hartford, CT.

CHAPTER III

GUN LORE OF THE OLD WEST

The weapons that played an important part in taming the Western frontier has always been a fascinating subject. Whether a gun enthusiast or not, there seems to be a compelling interest in the type of guns Western gunmen used, and just how well they handled them.

Perhaps my interest and curiosity has been more serious than that of the ordinary Western buff because of my involvement and participation as a Fast Draw competitor in this type sport, also writer and historian of the old West, as well as being a gun collector and shooter. As a member of The Roving Gunslingers Western Variety Show my part of the act is to perform most of the Western type gun tricks with the type of firearms that are credited as being used by the Western gunfighters in their exploited gun artistry. All of this has quite naturally inspired my interest and research into whether the frontier gunslingers really performed all the gun feats they are credited with or if it's just plain fantasy.

Styles change from year to year in stories about the gun feats of the old Western gunmen. One writer, or the writers of one period, tell tales that range from tall to utterly impossible, all sworn to as fact beyond question. Another writer, or the writers of another year, jump with calked boots on one of the impossible stories, disprove it, sneer at it, and leap from that to the conclusion that all the stories are false or even that there never was any such thing as a Western gunfighter, good or bad.

But there were men, more men than you know, because many of them never got or would not permit the publicity given to others who staked their lives on their gun skills, and some of those men survived too many such gambles to leave room for doubt that their skills were real. One writer "de-bunked" the whole gunfighter legend by stating that "such skill could not have been attained without long practice, and these men never practiced."

Who says they never practiced? Deputy Sheriff Breckinridge of the old Tombstone days practiced; he said so himself. Men who knew Billy the Kid say he practiced with rifle and revolver; that he dearly loved "a shooting match," for fun, and not so much for blood as was claimed. Wyatt Earp practiced; liked to let himself be "talked into" impromptu exhibitions of marksmanship, on the theory that men who saw him shoot might be dissuaded from challenging him in earnest. Wild Bill Hickok practiced; he enjoyed nothing better than an opportunity to display his gun handling expertness and marksmanship. This list could go on and on of the gunfighters who lived by the gun and sometimes died the same way, but who definitely realized the necessity of practice. They staked their lives on their gun skill, so why would they fail to develop that skill to the utmost? And anyway, guns were a part of the life of the era. The impromptu shooting match was as common as the impromptu horserace.

Men practiced endlessly for new ways to obtain better

accuracy or greater speed. Holsters and gun-hangers were invented, each calculated to give a man some "edge" in a gunfight. Guns of all types, from tiny derringers to sawed-off shotguns, were tried, touted, or discarded. Triggers of single action revolvers were removed or tied back, and "slip-hammers' added. Every top gunman insisted that speed was less important than making the first shot count, but every one of them worked to be able to make that first shot as sudden as possible, in a "sort of a slow hurry," to quote a phrase that became famous.

"Fanning" was tried, and discarded as a fighting method. Hardly a shot is fired in Hollywood epics that isn't "fanned," and every shot hits; that is in the movies. The Old Timers knew about fanning, but not a gunfighter of record used it in combat; it was too risky. Fanning a single action means the chances of failure are just too high when your life is in the balance.

The serious gun tricks performed in the Old West have always been a point of curiosity. One such trick is the "Curly Bill spin," sometimes called the "road agent spin." It has many variations, many "inventors." One story is that it originated with Curly Bill Brocius, a Tombstone bad man of considerable, even national, reputation. The story is told differently by each of its tellers, but one verson is that Tombstone Marshal Fred White got the drop on Curly Bill one day and demanded his gun. Curly presented the gun butt first, then spun it, fired and dropped Marshal White in his tracks.

Nobody knows now which of the several "spins" Curly used, if any. There are as many different methods as there are stories, or story tellers.

The spin could just as well have been called the "Hardin spin." In an alleged meeting (this story is at least as controversial as the Curly Bill one) between John Wesley Hardin and Wild Bill Hickok in 1871 at Abilene, Kansas. Hardin is supposed to have worked a spin against Hickok, but Hardin did not fire. Had he done so, Jack McCall, the eventual killer of Wild Bill, might never have achieved his niche in history.

The "Border shift" is another bit of legerdemain that earned notoriety in Fort Worth, Texas, in 1887. Jim Courtright and Luke Short were gunning for each other. Courtright was Marshal of Fort Worth, and Luke Short was a gambler and saloon keeper. Also Luke was a personal friend of such famous men as Wyatt Earp, Bat Masterson, and Doc Holliday. The feud between Courtright and Short came to shooting very quickly on the evening of February 8, 1887. Luke Short got his shot off first, and tore off Courtright's thumb. Desperately, Courtright tried to perform the juggling act called the "Border shift," which consists of tossing the gun from one hand to the other. But before the shift could be executed Luke Short pumped three more slugs into the Marshal.

The "Border shift" has been much practiced, with several variations, using one and two guns. The simple "Border shift" is nothing more than tossing the gun from one hand to the other in a level position. With two guns, it has been shown as a regular juggling act, tossing the guns in the air and spinning them at the same time.

It was a common practice of the old gunslinger to work over his pistol to give the "edge" in getting that first shot off. Almost invariably the gun would be the Colt Single Action Army revolver, sometimes known as the Frontier model. The design gave the gun perfect balance, easy to draw and handle. Its large hammer made for easy cocking, the grip would just about fit any hand, and the small trigger guard made for easy spinning. Among the numerous alterations committed by the gunman to this weapon were, filing off part of the trigger guard, removing the trigger or tieing it back, replacing the hammer with a Bisley Colt hammer for better thumb traction. They weakened the hammer spring, and they removed the front sight "to keep it from snagging in the holster."

One unique idea for carrying a gun without a holster was used by the famous Texas Ranger, Jim Gillett. A metal plate was slotted and riveted to a belt, and the hammer screw of the Colt Single Action was replaced with a large-headed screw that fitted into the T slot in the plate. The pistol was pushed back until the large headed screw would fall into a slight depression at the rear of the slot. The gun would hang there and swing easily. To shoot the gun, it could be removed from the slot or simply pivoted and fired.

The famous OK Corral shootout depicted in an artist's rendering on cloth. Colts, Winchester rifle and sawed-off shotgun were all being used by the gunfighters shown.

Author George Virgines, as a member of the Roving Gunslingers
Wild West Show, demonstrates fancy juggling of the border shift
with two guns.

A collection of Old West Weapons from top: Colt single action Army revolver; sawed-off double barrel shotgun, and Winchester M1873 saddle-ring carbine, caliber .44-40.

31

The most famous handgun of the Old West, the Colt single action Army revolver. It was in every arsenal of guns whether used by lawman or outlaw.

A couple of gunslingers ready for action. Jack Anderson, left, said to be a friend of Wild Bill Hickok, holds a Colt single action revolver and carries a Bowie knife in his belt. His friend, Yankee Judd, holds a rifle at the ready. He also has a holstered six-shooter and a Bowie knife in his belt. The photograph was made in Leadville, Colorado, in 1879.

A pair of "Gambler" specials or hide-away guns — Colt Deringers. Left: Fourth Model Cal. 22, a new version of the original .41 caliber. Right: New Model 7 shot Caliber .22.

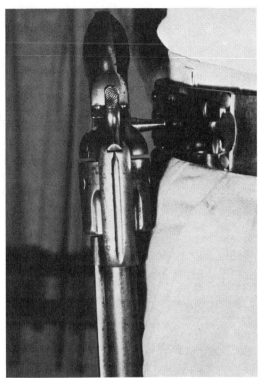

A Colt single action revolver equipped with a large hammer screw which fits into a slotted metal plate attached to the belt.

The unique slotted metal plate which is riveted to a belt. The large hammer screw of the Colt single action revolver fitted into the slot. Famous Texas Ranger Jim Gillet is said to have used this type gun.

John Wesley Hardin, gunfighter from Texas, designed what he called a "holster-vest," later called the "Hardin vest." It was a skeleton-type vest, made from calfskin, and it had two holster pockets slanting toward the front. The guns were carried with the butts forward for a cross draw. But this vest never gained any popularity with the gunslingers.

Another type of trick holster that never reached any degree of popularity was the swivel type. The holster was attached to the belt by means of a leather tab and a swiveling rivet. All the gunman had to do was to push the pistol butt down and bring up the barrel and fire through an opening at the bottom of the holster. Like the slot-and-stud naked-gun carry of Jim Gillett, this pivoted holster limited the area of firing, preventing a shot to the left or right.

Gunmen were an ingenious lot. Ben Thompson, another Texan, according to tradition, invented the shoulder holster which could be worn under the coat and conceal the weapon. This style holster is still popular today, and many variations and improvements have been made to suit individual taste.

Dallas Stoudenmire, a two gun marshall of El Paso, Texas, simplified the carrying of two guns by having leather-lined hip pockets tailored into his pants. The story goes that he could produce his six-shooters from these pockets with lightning speed.

The "gambler's special," the hide-away or hold-out gun as it was sometimes called, was the small single or double barrel derringer. Some fairly well known characters admitted that they never felt fully dressed without a hide-away gun or two. Ladies of pleasure were apt to have a derringer tucked away somewhere, for emergencies. Remington's double barrel, over and under, caliber .41 rimfire was perhaps the most frequently used as a hold-out gun. In one instance, a peace officer in Arizona is credited with carrying eleven small but lethal derringers concealed on his person, and one knife! This walking arsenal had his weapons so distributed that, to the ordinary observer, he appeared unarmed.

The other extreme in choice of weapons carried by gunmen, good or bad, was the sawed-off double barrel shotgun. To list the celebrated gunmen who used the shotgun in their profession would read like a "Who's Who" in Western history. The roll call could be answered by such men as Doc Holliday, Wyatt Earp, Wild Bill Hickok, Pat Garrett, and Jesse James. Shotguns were in the arsenals of such organizations as Wells Fargo, Adams Express, the Pinkertons, and the Rangers. The standard shotgun, a 10 gauge double barrel, was sawed off to 18 or 20 inches, and loaded with No. 00 shot. No gunmen's arsenal was complete without one.

The lethal effect of the scatter gun, as it was known sometimes, at close range was devastating. It was by far the "meanest" gun used in the West. A gunslinger thought twice before risking a showdown against a shotgun. On the side of the law, "riding shotgun" is synonymous with Wells Fargo. It was a hard and dangerous task and the company selected its men with care. The shotgun messenger who rode with the stage is credited with discouraging many a highwayman's ambition for a fast buck. A man with a shotgun was the deadliest man in the West.

Many different types and models of guns were used on the frontier besides the Colt Single Action revolver. There were various other model Colt handguns. Also the Smith & Wesson, Remington, Forehand & Wadsworth, and Merwin Hulbert revolvers. In the rifle line there were the Kentucky and Hawken rifles, Springfield, Remington, Henry, and the ever famous Winchester.

No self respecting cowhand, frontiersman, or gunfighter would cross the country without a Winchester rifle or carbine tucked away in a saddle-scabbard. The Winchester Saddle Carbine was perhaps the most popular rifle in the West, and is, even today. It was available in the popular calibers of .32-20, .38-40, and .44-40, which made it a companion firearm to the Colt Single Action revolver that also was manufactured in the same calibers. Of course both weapons were made in a variety of other calibers.

The West also had its share of sneaky gunmen. This type of gunmen who was unable to outdraw, outshoot, or out-bluff his opponent and so waited his chance to shoot the unsuspecting victim in the back or bushwack him. He wasn't fussy. Some of our most celebrated Westerners met their demise in this fashion. Wild Bill Hickok was shot in the back by Jack McCall in Deadwood, South Dakota; Billy the Kid was shot and killed in a dark room in New Mexico; Pat Garrett, the man who was given credit for shooting Billy, was ambushed in 1908 while carrying a shotgun in his buggy that he never got to put into play; and Bob Ford, the never to be forgotten "dirty little coward who shot Mr. Howard," used less than heroic tactics when he killed Jesse James at St. Joseph, Missouri. No matter what side of the law you were on in those days, it was good life insurance to watch over your shoulder. You never knew when some sneaky gunman might try to enhance his reputation or fatten his pocketbook with reward money.

When all is said and done, these leather slapping gunslingers, good or bad, all contributed in their way to the gun lore and legend of the Old West.

BIBLIOGRAPHY

The American Gun — Gummer — 1961.
"Triggernometry" *By Eugene Cunningham.*
"Fast & Fancy Shooting" *by Ed McGivern.*
Gun Digest Treasury — 1956.
Gun Digest — 1959.

CHAPTER IV

CANVAS LAWMEN

The Western lawman has been the source of more interest and controversy than any other type of frontiersman. He has been the most maligned or the most admired, depending on which side of the fence you might be.

On the frontier he had to be a one man police force and often as not, the judge, jury, and executioner. The position, in those days, certainly wasn't exactly enticing considering that they were under-paid, over-worked, and a constant target for some gunman. At best, law enforcement on the frontier was both primitive and bloody.

So the lawman emerged as a legendary figure and became an excellent subject to be captured on canvas of the masters, old and new, of Western art.

Call them what you may, City Marshal, Sheriff, Texas or Arizona Ranger, U.S. Marshal, Indian Police, or just police, they all helped mould what was to become formal law in the settlement of the West.

Writers and historians all shared in their efforts to seek out the legendary figures who subdued the violence that once was prevalent across the frontier. It wasn't until later years that photographs of some of the famous lawmen began to appear in publications. So, unless he is an avid Western America buff, the average Western fan accepts the look of a frontier lawman from the movies. This medium also depicted many costume changes of the frontier lawman. Old time cinema stars such as William S. Hart, Billy Anderson, William Farnum, and others, were presented in a realistic, down to the last detail of sweat and grime, look of the old West. Then in the years of the thirties and fourties, the Western movie hero such as Roy Rogers, Tom Mix, Ken Maynard, Gene Autry, Rex Allen, and many more became great stars. Their approach to dress became distinctive in design and style, bordering on almost a circus uniform.

Now, as the movies go through another era, the Western lawmen and frontiersmen are being presented more realistically. John Wayne was perhaps one of the all time greats among Western stars who has contributed more toward keeping the Western image believable, entertaining, and our Western heritage alive.

But to turn back the pages of history, one has to pay high tribute to the Western artists of yesteryear. They are the ones who have captured the spirit and color of our West on canvas and have preserved it for future generations to admire, study, and remember.

The list of the many famous artists who have painted the early West and its people is quite long and only a few can be mentioned here.

The past works of such famous artists as Charles M. Russell, Frederick Remington, N. C. Wyeth, E. A. Burbank, O. C. Seltzer, and others have been displayed in galleries and museums. One other artist, now deceased, whose work in the field of Western art is gaining great recognition, is W. H. D.

42

Koerner. This fine artist was noted for his great illustrations for the covers and stories of the Saturday Evening Post. Many of his paintings depicted the lawman in various forms of action with such titles as "The Evidence", "The Troublemaker", "Shotgun and the Law", "Deputy", "The Posse - Law In Action", and "Sheriff and Citizens of the Law", to name a few.

All of the above artists have had reams written and their paintings illustrated in many books and magazines, so their work is familiar to most people.

Today, the popularity of Western art is fantastic, to say the least. Although the paintings of the past distinguished masters are just about untouchable in price, the art of lessor publicized artists of early years is fast becoming prominent in reputation and artistic value.

Another breed of collector who has become most interested in Western art are the many firearm collectors of Colts, Smith & Wessons, Remington, Winchesters, and the many other available and collectable guns. Once again it is the lawman who has become such a colorful subject of Western art and has created much interest in these arms. These "Canvas Lawmen", and in sculpture, have done their part to enhance the heroic stature of the badge-toters. Many gun collectors have come to realize the importance and interest of collecting in areas related to their main field. And a common denominator can also be found in those works of art where the artist has chosen as his subject, or included in it, weapons, belt-holsters, buckles, knives, clubs, medals, or badges. The combining of arms and accroutrements with painting, sculpture, or other art forms gives the greatest pleasure and interest to Western art and arms collectors.

So with the above thought in mind, in researching and viewing Western art, I noted that the characters portrayed almost always included a frontier lawman, I thought it would be interesting to compare a few of the Western artists of yesteryear with the Western artists of today, especially their interpretation of a frontier lawman.

Charles M. Russell was perhaps one of the greatest of Western artists. He had lived during the harsh times of early Montana and saw first hand all of the characters that made up frontier life. In one of his colorful paintings of 1914 entitled "The Call of The Law" he depicts the "Canvas Lawman" on horseback wearing the heavy clothes of a cold Montana and displaying his badge with one hand and holding a Winchester on a pair of surprised law breakers. Russell worked as a cowboy on cattle ranches in Montana and could have witnessed a scene like this. Every detail is captured in this picture, from the Bull-Durham bag hanging from the pocket of one of the outlaws to the complete surprise on their faces.

Another famous artist whose illustrations have contributed greatly toward preserving the feel of the old West is Newell Converse Wyeth, who could be called the "Painter of Men in Action." His technique and talent captured a real atmosphere of the wild west in each of his paintings. Even his many illustrations that appeared in Scribner's, Harper's, Collier's, McClure's, and many books are now becoming great collector's items. When you speak of N. C. Wyeth you are speaking of a famous family of artists. His son Andrew is a distinguished and famous artist of today. His daughter Henrietta (Mrs. Peter Hurd) is held in high esteem internationally for her portraits and of course, her husband is the famous New Mexico painter, muralist, lithographer, and illustrator, Peter Hurd.

N. C. Wyeth was a dedicated painter, and he too, lived the Western roles he depicted on canvas. One of his dramatic paintings of a frontier marshal and his posse is a fine example of his interpretation of a Western lawman. This was painted in 1907 to illustrate the book "Langford of The Three Bars" by Kate and Virgil D. Boyles. Looking at it you can almost feel and taste the alkaline dust kicked up by the possemen's horses.

The list of past talented artists could go on and on who have portrayed the West and its lawmen on canvas. Their works are well preserved throughout the country in museums and private collections.

Today a new breed of Western artists are lending their talents in displaying today and yesterday's West. In a way, they

"Arizona Ranger" is the title of this forceful looking lawman of the Old West. It was painted by prominently known artist Robert J. Moore of Colorado. Original 1972.

A pewter sculpture, "Texas Ranger Trackin'", was done by Philip Kraczkowski in 1972 and presented by Worchester Pewter one of a series of "The American Frontier". It measures 5 x 5 inches.

"Man With a Star", bronze sculpture by Ernest E. Caviness, 1976. It is No. 15 of 50 originals. This old marshal loading his shotgun is typical of the accuracy created in Caviness' work.

W.H.D. Koerner (1878-1938)

Ruth Koerner Oliver

Illustration by N. C. Wyeth from the book "Langford of the 3-Bars" by Kate and Virgil D. Boyles — 1907.

"Chief of Police", a watercolor rendering by Julia B. Collins, noted portrait artist of Wisconsin. The subject is William M. Tilghman, police chief of Oklahoma City in 1911.

"The Badge Toter", a pen and ink color by popular and talented artist Ernest Lisle Reedstrom of Cedar Lake, Indiana. This fine interpretation of a lawman can be judged by the meticulous attention to detail.

51

have taken on a task that presents different problems from the past masters. First, they have striven for originality and not let the art of Russell, Weyth, Koerner, and others affect their style or technique. The successful artist of today has to research with photographs, artifacts, and a collection of assorted Western relics to depict any scene or character of the early frontier. The proof that the contemporary artist has accomplished this can be seen at the many museums, galleries, and private collections that exhibit their work.

One of the most unique, interesting, and contemporary pieces of lawmen art, that today, could be classified as Western Americana art work, was actually done by an old time New Mexico lawman, Fred Lambert. After serving almost a life time in law enforcement, he was 84 years old when he passed away in 1971. He directed his talents toward writing, illustrating, and painting. His book "Bygone Days of the Old West" is not only interesting but demonstrated his fine technique in pen and ink sketching. To this author he presented an original piece of colorful art work entitled "Guns Old and New" that depicted his favorite Colt Six-Shooter, badge, holsters and belt, and a pair of horsemen. The arrangement of the subjects in the picture are off balance, but the detail very sharp and good, it could be called crude but still very unique, and the subjects and items are certainly Western Americana.

The rendering of an old time and forceful looking character depicting an Arizona Ranger in which his badge and Colt gun is prominently displayed was done by Robert J. Moore of Colorado. Bob is an ex-rodeo rider who after several broken bones decided that the comfort and love of his art was a bit more gentle. He is a self-taught artist who is a real stickler for authenticity and spends many hours researching and studying the old West and its history. This type of dedication to background and detail has made his art in much demand and is in museums and collections all over the country.

An artist who is fast becoming more well known and respected for his authentic paintings and book illustrations of the Civil War and the early Western frontier is writer and illustrator, Ernest Lisle Reedstrom of Cedar Lake, Indiana. His work is outstanding in every artistic medium and his attention and knowledge for detail give his art added significance.

Reedstrom's pen and ink, color sketch presentation of a lawman shown here is clearly original. His choice is unique and fresh. Much research is reflected in the clothing and dress of this frontier character. Note the coat, vest, tie, hat, and especially the badge and firearms, all show the astute attention given to details. This is characteristic of Reedstrom's artistic talent. This painting was executed exclusively for this author and book by Reedstrom and is the first time ever published. Reedstrom is a meticulous researcher and his own painting of "Custer's Last Campaign" a 60 x 45 inch canvas involved five years of research and three years to paint, has been accepted by many prominent authorities as one of the most authentic depictions of this famous battle. He has done some remarkable illustrations for such authors as Lawrence A. Frost of "The Custer Album", Fairfax Downey of "Fife, Drum and Bugle", Carl W. Breihan of "The Complete Authentic Life of Jesse James". He also did the jacket design, end sheets, and chapter art for Dale T. Schoenberger's book "The Gunfighters". And of course, he illustrated this author's own book, "Saga of The Colt Six-Shooter". In 1978 Reedstrom won the Spur Award from the Western Writers of America for his own fine book, "Bugles, Banners, and War Bonnets:.

Last, but certainly not least, is the truly fine portrait art contributed by Julia B. Collins of Wisconsin, exclusively for this book and a first time to be published. For her subject she chose a famous and noted lawman of Western frontier history, William M. Tilghman. His background is the subject of many books, newspaper and magazine articles, and movies. He is a true part of the old West.

This painting depicts Tilghman when he was the Chief of Police of Oklahoma City, Oklahoma in 1911. Note the absolute faithfulness Julia has given to the details of his uniform, such as the gold embroidery hat badge; and the button markings of police.

When interviewed Julia made the following statement about her feelings in interpreting this old lawman: "It was a real challenge that leaned toward frustration — Chief Tilghman has a curious face with enormously clear, piercing eyes (steel blue) which seem to create a very powerful presence that I was striving to capture. After reading the background of this man, I think the Chief might have done the country a great service by exterminating more outlaws and fewer buffalo."

Julia Collins, is what may be termed a natural artist. Since childhood she has leaned toward art. She has worked for an advertising firm and for many years, according to her, "to pad the till" with extra income, did logos, letterheads, leaded glass creations, and of course paintings and portraits too numerous to mention. She has worked with pastels, pencils, oils, charcoal, and finally water colors. This is her favorite medium and as the painting of Tilghman displays, a very apt choice. People and animals are her first love as subjects and fine examples are prized possessions in many private collections throughout the country.

Although this narrative has dealt mainly with original paintings it would be a mistake to think of art as simply paintings. The creative endeavors of an artist knows no boundaries, and can be expressed in a variety of objects and materials. Art needn't mean originals, either. In addition to paintings, lithographs and prints can be found in many cases at lower prices. While some sculpture is available in precious metals, it is also to be found in bronze, copper, pewter, ceramic, wood, and other materials, with prices set accordingly. There are museum quality sculptures available inexpensive materials that would enhance any collection. And any work of art by unknown artist may become a valued heirloom of the future. Note the work of two fine sculptures illustrated, one in bronze, the other pewter.

It has been only in recent years that art collectors have become appreciative of the endeavors of Western artists of yesteryear and especially today.

Each artist has approached the subject in a different and unique way. The end results show clearly that they all possess a major talent that is certain to grow as time goes by. All are fine art accomplishments worthy of the severest critic's consideration. Their dedication and their talents have given the West, past and present, new distinction.

BIBLIOGRAPHY

Ernest Lisle Reedstrom — Indiana
Julia B. Collins — Wisconsin
Robert J. Moore — Colorado
Fred Lambert — New Mexico

CHAPTER V

PRESENTING
LEGEND MAKER
STAN LYNDE

Many names, places, and people have contributed to the history of the "Old West". Added to this are the many authors and artists who have recorded for posterity, their manuscripts and canvases depicting what life on the frontier was really like. The authors are many and such famous artists as Russell, Remington, Koerner, and Wyeth, to name a very few, are synonymous with our frontier history education.

In a lighter vein but still cognizant of the early West were many cartoonists who were exponents of the wild and woolly West. Such names as J. R. Williams, the creator of "Out Our

Way". Fred Harman whose character "Red Ryder" was a famous and popular western strip for many years. The list could go on and on of the many artists whose cartoon strips, and later comic books, could be titled "Comics of The American West".

In the last few decades another name has been added to the roster of talented artist/writers and contributors to fine western art cartoons, his name, Stan Lynde. He is a traditional Westerner and his first contribution to Western lore was the creation of one of the most popular and unique cartoon strips appropriately named "Rick O'Shay" marshal of "Conniption." "Rick O'Shay" was born and appeared in newspapers on April 27, 1958, which was syndicated by the Chicago Tribune-New York News Syndicate, Inc. This picturesque Western cartoon character, plus the most accurate Western scenes, was read and enjoyed by millions of newspaper readers throughout the United States, Canada, Europe, Australia, Philippines, and South America.

The humor and accuracy of the strip was in a relaxing tempo of the early West. The main characters consist of "Rick O'Shay", an amiable young fellow who is the town marshal; a gunfighter with the timely name of "Hipshot Percussion", based on an old gunfighter that was an acquaintance of Stan Lynde as a youngster. Other characters and citizens of "Conniption" who made a steady procession through the strip also had quaint names such as "Gaye Abandon", the girl interest, who owns the local saloon; "Deuces Wild", the major and tinhorn gambler; "Basil Metabolism", a doctor who patches up the many injured; "Chief Horses Neck", the well adjusted Indian Chief; a Mexican cowboy, "Manuel Labor", who is deputy marshal, and many others.

The cast and the strip were humorous, while the situations were believable; Stan Lynde had created a mixture of Western images that had the quality of authenticity.

Stan Lynde, a natural westerner hales from Lodge Grass, Montana, which is a part of the Crow Indian reservation and not very far from the historic site of Custer's battle field. Stan grew up in this country that was as wild and woolly as any part of the old West could be. The town of Lodge Grass was the pattern for the cartoon town "Conniption." It had no electricity, telephone or other modern conveniences during the time Stan was growing up there. It was here that he learned to ride a bronc and shoot on the Mill Iron Ranch were his father worked for Harvey Willcut. His father was in partnership with the great Antler Ranch, a livestock operation which ran more than 100,000 sheet and about 50,000 cattle.

From his mother, Stan was encouraged to draw and the desire to become a cartoonist came early. His mother was artistically talented which was an advantage to this budding artist.

Stan Lynde went through the usual education process of high school, Montana State University, a hitch in the navy during the Korean War, and later worked in various parts of the country, ending up in New York. After a great deal of trial and error with cartooning, "Rick O'Shay" was born in 1958. The cartoon legend of "Rick O'Shay" was to last for twenty years. This was an ambition fulfilled for Stan, because he always wanted to do a Western and historical strip. He has his heart in the West and "Rick O'Shay" was his first love. Stan gives meticulous attention to his strip; the furniture, clothing, firearms and equipment are drawn from the actual articles. The realism even extends to the cattle brands which are real and registered brands of ranchers in Yellowstone and Big Horn counties.

The firearms are especially accurate. Stan uses real guns in all cases for the art and accuracy in the strip, and this is what he constantly strives for in their portrayal. Sometimes he uses models posing as gunfighters, but often works from photographs and source books.

Stan has a small collection of firearms that he not only uses for his art work but also enjoys shooting. His favorite for deer and antelope hunting is the Model 94 Winchester, in .30-30 caliber. This still is the favorite saddle gun among Westerners who ride. His other favorite is a Ruger single action .22 handgun that he uses to practice fast draw. Incidently, Stan as a good Westerner, prefers the single action type gun to the double action or automatic. He is a real traditionalist.

The demands of producing a cartoon strip and making deadlines prevents Stan from doing as much shooting as he would like to do, but he still manages to break away for hunting and target practice. Shooting remains as one of his favorite sports. Besides, Stan believes the more shooting he does the better his cartoon representations of shooting will be, and that all knowledge possessed by a cartoonist is reflected in his work.

The picturesque landscapes used in the strip are also drawn from life. All he has to do is look outside his windows from his home in Montana, and see plenty of fine inspiring Western scenery that finds its way into his strips.

In 1977 came the bad news for all "Rick O'Shay" fans that Stan Lynde had decided to retire from producing this most popular Western strip. It was a difficult decision for Stan, knowing of his love and dedication to the strip for almost twenty years. The problem was mainly an economic one, but like they say, "All good things sometimes have to come to an end." However, "Rick O'Shay" was guided by new hands, two fine artist/authors, Mel Keeper and Marian J. Dern, later Alfedo P. Alcala. But the strip lacked that certain Stan Lynde touch.

With the demise of Stan's favorite vocation and love, he turned to other projects such as magazine articles, illustrating, speaking arrangements, and oil painting. Most of all there was more time to share with his family which included his wonderful and talented wife, Sidne, who in her own right is a writer, painter, photographer, and a working woman as an editorial assistant on the Carbon County, Montana, News. One of the unique story books she and Stan turned out in 1975 was entitled "Calamity Jane". Sidne did the excellent job on the prose and Stan on the colorful art work. Stan and Sidne have three sons, Mark, Richard, and Taylor, all of whom have artistic talents that had to rub off from very talented parents.

On June 24, 1979, a new and exciting western character by the name of "Latigo" was introduced and created by Stan Lynde for the Field Newspaper Syndicate. This much needed and sought after western strip is featured in newspapers all over

Author George Virgines demonstrates some six-shooter technique to cartoonist/artist Stan Lynde. *Chicago Tribune*

A replica of "Rick O'Shay's" badge presented to the author by Stan Lynde.

Stan Lynde, left, presenting an original "Rick O'Shay" cartoon to the author at a fast draw contest.

"Latigo", a forceful and exciting hero created by Stan Lynde.
Field Enterprises

Two of Stan Lynde's original and popular cartoon characters.
"Rick O'Shay", left, and "Hipshot Percussion".

Chicago Tribune-New York News Syndicate

Stan Lynde at his drawing board completing a strip on his famous and popular cartoon character, "Latigo".

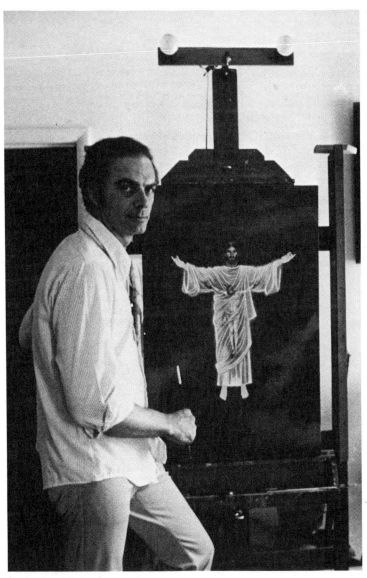

A more serious aspect of Stan Lynde's artistic talent is depicted here in his painting of Jesus Christ.

the United States, Europe, Latin and South America. The strip is set in the post- Civil War period of the American West. It contains all the standard ingredients necessary in a good western series such as a strong identifiable characters, authenticity and that meticulous detail for which Stan is so well noted. It also contains a cast of unique and interesting personalities that Stan has so adeptly developed in his western strips. The strip's main hero is, of course, Cole "Latigo Cantrell", Marshal of the town of "Rimfire", and as such is a strong and courageous defender of justice. Some of the other characters are "Dark Star" — a beautiful Crow Indian medicine woman; "Duke Sateen", a professional gambler; "Claudious Max", the villain, and "Jordan Rivers" is "Rimfire's" Christian minister, who will be a strong member of the cast. There are others, all of whom should make this strip a great western adventure series.

Stan Lynde has become a legend maker, first with "Rick O'Shay" and now "Latigo".

REFERENCES

Correspondence and interviews with Stan Lynde — Red Lodge, Montana

Cartoonist Profiles Magazine — Winter 1969 — June 1979 — 1981.

Guns Magazine May 1972 — *Marshal Rick O'Shay" by G. E. Virgines*

CHAPTER VI

BADGES AND BADGE TOTERS

That bright, shiny piece of metal which adorned a Western lawman's uniform now hangs in a relics collector's den. The demand for star and shield badges has become so great that the "fast-buck" boys are producing and selling reproductions and, what is worse, asking outrageous prices for them.

For the collector there exists a range of specialization of police, sheriff, marshal, ranger, or constable badges. Another possibility is to collect a badge from every state in the Union or specialize in those from one's own state.

Not every lawman in the old West had a badge. And many of the old Western badges never were inscribed with town, county, or state names. They were just plainly marked

71

"Sheriff" or "Deputy" or just plain "Police". Badges inscribed with historic town names are indeed scarce.

Several years ago a badge collector who was fortunate enough to have a collection of early historic Western lawman badges decided to have a set of replicas made. These were very substantial and realistic badges in star and shield designs were sold for $3.50 each. This was about in 1959-'60. They were marked with such names as Deputy Marshal — Tombstone; Deputy Sheriff — Cheyenne; Marshal — Dodge City; Marshal — Pecos, Texas; Deputy Marshal — Abilene, Kansas; Marshal — Topeka; Deputy Marshal — Laramie; Marshal — Dead-wood; Deputy Sheriff — Hangtown; and Wells Fargo — Special Agent. These badges were very impressive in appearance but all were clearly stamped on the obverse side "Replica" and described, advertised, and sold as such. But through the years these original replicas have been advertised and sold at prices ranging from $50 and up — whatever the market will bear. What is worse they are not advertised or marked replicas. It should be mentioned that the original replicas were only produced in a very limited quantity. Some of them have turned up with the marking "Replica" filed off. Collectors, take heed and beware!

Other badges which have been copies and passed off as originals are the Texas Ranger and Wells Fargo type badges.

Badges manufacturing companies were in business as early as 1868. Others produced badges in 1879, 1884, 1886, and 1888, and on upward. Their catalogs are sometimes a good source for identifying old designs but not necessary authenticating a particular badge relating to a specific city or town. A lot of badges illustrated are just sample pieces. One other item of interest concerning badge companies is that they have very little to offer on the history of individual badges. They also frown on selling any old, obsolete badges they may have.

One old badge maker did state that they had a traveling salesman who carried a case with various styles of blank badges, a punch letter and number set, tools and chart of the lettering available. He would tour police stations and sheriff's offices and make the badges right on the spot.

Today, badges of peace officers can be found in every size,

72

shape, and form. Stars are in 5,6,7,8, and even 9 points, with and without ball tips on the points. Some stars are surrounded by a circle or wreath, or cut out in a shield, or in a sun-burst type pattern. The shield type badge is also a popular style with the familiar spread eagle adorning the top of the shield. Copper and brass was a common material used for badges of the early police forces.

An old-time jeweler's catalog dating to 1900 advertised police, sheriff, and city marshal badges in star or shield designs. They were offered in nickel plate, German silver, and were engraved according to the customers' wishes. The price was $1.50 and up.

Badges in a variety of shapes and designs were made from gold, silver, steel, copper, brass, even leather and tin. A type particularly interesting to the collector was fashioned from various types of coins. Practically from the time of coinage it was popular to have various types of jewelry made from gold and silver coins. There are bracelets, rings, earrings, brooches, pins, spoons, cufflinks, and many other decorate ornaments made from coins. So it is natural that there would be law enforcement badges made from coins.

The Texas Rangers were such a law enforcement outfit that took a Mexican silver Peso type coin and had a five-point star inside circle carved from it to make up their famous badge. Other old Western type badges were fashioned from our silver dollar. The best of all, however, were those cut from solid gold or silver, ornately engraved, and adorned with diamonds, rubies, and other gems. These prize items were reserved for ceremonial presentation from either fellow officers or neighbors. The local jeweler was usually called upon to make this type of special badge.

One special badge was described in the Globe newspaper, May 6, 1884. This fine badge, costing $40 was presented to City Marshal Bill Tilghman. It was solid gold and engraved on the face, "Wm. Tilghman, City Marshal", and on the reverse side, "Presented by your friends, May 2, 1884". He was a great lawman who was a credit to his profession.

Another fine example of the jeweler's artistry and craftsmanship was noted in Nov. 16, 1906, in the Mobile,

Alabama newspaper. In part it mentioned in large type "Sheriff Powers — Presented with a handsome badge by members of the force — Judge J. E. Alford with the sheriff's deputies presented to Sheriff John F. Powers a beautifully enameled badge that bears the words 'John F. Powers, Sheriff Mobile County'". This most unique shield type badge was of solid gold with a white French enamel face and the name and State Seal of Alabama engraved through the enamel onto the gold background.

The name "Tin Star" was a slang expression from the frontier depicting the local peace officer. When there was no other source to obtain a badge, oftener than not, the sheriff or marshal, bound and determined he was going to wear a badge to show off his authority, fashioned his own out of the cheapest and most plentiful material around, namely from the old tin can. There was an endless supply on every garbage dump. Hence the nick-name "Tin Star."

The quest for the law-enforcement type badges has definitely become a very popular collector specialization. But what has inspired this fascinating pasttime and hobby is the history that is associated with each one of these varied shaped stars, shields, and badges of the badge toters.

For example, the many types of badges associated with the most famous police force in the world, is that of the Texas Rangers, and their badges follow their legendary history. Reams have been written about the heroic deeds and the flamboyant personalities that made Ranger history. The type of badge that the ranger first wore and how it got its start in Texas is little known. One story has it that one ranger took a Mexican silver Peso coin and carved a badge from it for himself. The idea caught on and before long many rangers adopted the idea.

In October, 1962, the Director of the Texas Department of Safety and Chief of the Texas Rangers, Colonel Homer Garrison, Jr., announced that the Texas Rangers were once again going to change their badges to the original and traditional design of the carved Mexican five Peso silver coin engraved five point star in a cut-out circle type badge worn by their predecessors during the frontier days.

Unique presentation badge made from copper and brass and engraved to Chas. Fred Lambert of Cimmaron, New Mexico. Circa 1900.

Dept. of Public Safety — "CO D" Texas Rangers cutout from an old original Mexican silver type Peso coin.

Shown in its original case, Powers' presentation badge appears as "presented by the Deputies of Mobile County," in gold letters and so marked in the case. The badge is solid gold with French enamel face and State seal in colors. Circa 1906.

Sheriff John F. Powers of Mobile, Alabama, was the recipient of a fine gold presentation badge (Right). Circa 1906.

Possibly a replacement badge for a Ranger. This one is inscribed on the back "Ray Myles — No. 11". Circa 1900.

An example of the popular circle and cutout star badge in sterling and so marked on the reverse. This particular badge has been pictured in Colt Sheriff's model ads that appeared in almost all gun magazines distributed in the country. Circa 1980-'81.

Author George Virgines personal issued badge as a Deputy Sheriff of Lincoln County, New Mexico.

A plainly marked police star buckle and whistle as worn by Indian policemen.

This old deputy U.S. Marshal badge came from Texas and is
carved out of a silver Mexican coin. Circa 1900.

GEV Collection

Author and deputy sheriff, George Virgines stands with an array
of stars and shields mounted in displays.

Replica badges of frontier towns.

Another Ranger Force, shorter lived, hence less celebrated than the Texas Rangers is the Arizona Rangers, nonetheless distinguished by heroic deed and sensational exploits. This famed force of crime fighters, organized in 1901, and lasting until 1909, drove organized banditry from the territory and their silver star was worn as a badge of honor. It was just a modest silver star type badge with five points, ball tipped with a slight engraving on the edges, the trooper's number or rank at the top and the name "Arizona Rangers".

Today most people identify the U.S. Marshal with the glowing legends of the old West. This is true because the names of the men who served as marshals and deputies of the United States reads like "Who's Who" in frontier history. There are names like Bill Tilghman, Heck Thomas, Cris Madsen, Frank Dalton, Virgil Earp, Bat Masterson, and Frank M. Canton, just to name a very few. They were men who became legends in their own time because they were living in a period when lawlessness was widespread and courage and badge toters went hand in hand.

The United States Marshal badge is symbolic of a very important law enforcement agency of our government and of great legends. They wore a variety of badges.

A little less known law agency, but just as important is the Indian Police. Their laws and law enforcement for their people was perhaps very complex, but it brought the American Indian's concept of law enforcement and the white man's into a workable legal system. It was in the 1860's and 1870's that the Indian Police began. Any badge pertaining to this police force would certainly be of historic significance, even the present day police force. Of the badges that represented this law group, the officer's badge was a large shiny 6 point star, with just the simple inscription "Police". For the non-coms or privates a plain shield sufficed. Earlier badges were of the shield type with stars across the top to signify rank. Like the U.S. Marshal they wore a variety of design stars and shields. Collectors have to be very careful in this particular field as there are many fake pieces circulating about.

Regardless of the shape or material of these many badges, the important thing was the mettle of the badge toters who wore them. The badges represent many things: our frontier history; various law enforcement agencies; the legal systems that help to civilize our country; and identify the men who were known as the "Badge Toters" — up to include the present day.

As this hobby of collecting symbols of the lawman becomes more popular more museums, historical societies, and as more law enforcement agencies begin to recognize their historic heritage, more displays of badges are becoming apparent. All of this contributes to the significance and interest in the history of our law enforcement.

BIBLIOGRAPHY

"Badges of Law and Order" *by George E. Virgines*

CHAPTER VII

MEMENTOS OF THE 101
WILD WEST SHOW

Galloping horses, twirling ropes, and the blast of gunfire made the old Wild West show a colorful and glamorous spectacle that thrilled a generation of Americans, few of whom ever saw a working cowboy or a mounted Indian but to whom these shows brought the thrill and excitement of the frontier.

Gone are the flamboyant figures who put together these fabulous shows and travelled with them to all parts of the country, and even to Europe. Men such as Colonel "Buffalo Bill" Cody, "Pawnee Bill" Lillie, Colonel Cummins, and the Miller brothers.

Outstanding among these men were the Miller brothers

of Marland, Oklahoma, whose 101 Ranch Real Wild West Show was most popular between 1908 and 1914. It was revived in 1925 and continued in existence until 1932. An attempt to revive it in 1945 was short lived and the show folded for all time in 1946.

The Miller brothers — Joseph, George, and Zack — were pioneer cattlemen in Oklahoma's Cherokee Strip. Their ranch was a virtual empire and covered more than 100,000 acres. Here they ran huge herds of cattle that required a small army of cowboys. It was here, also, that they organized and brought into being their now legendary 101 Ranch Wild West Show, named after the ranch and its 101 brand. The show was later combined with a circus and among those who, at one time or another, travelled with it were such men as Buffalo Bill, Jess Willard — the noted champion boxer, Tom Mix, Buck Jones, and Jack Hoxie, all of whom became famous western movie stars.

During its day, the 101 Ranch Wild West Show scattered mementos of its existence — posters, programs, tickets, photographs, buttons, postcards, firearms, and a host of other souvenirs — far and wide. Many of these can still be found by anyone interested enough to hunt them out.

The 101 brand used by the Miller brothers became their coat of arms. They not only branded their cattle and horses with it but also used it to decorate their equipment and to embellish stationary, posters, coins, badges, even silverware and dishes. If a saddle, bridle, belt, buckle or firearm bears a 101 marking the chances are it originated with the 101 Ranch and Wild West Show.

There are two known preserved, unique saddles that once belonged to Joe and Zack Miller. Zack had a very ornate and carved leather, silver decorated saddle and it was last known to have been exhibited at the Texas Ranger Museum in Waco, Texas. A more exquisite saddle once belonging to Joe Miller is on display at the Wollaroc Museum in Bartlesville, Oklahoma. This particular saddle has the distinction as having been advertised as "The World's Finest Saddle" and described in part as follows: "$10,000 saddle made for J. C. Miller of the 101 Ranch Wild West Show by S. D. Myres,

Sweetwater, Texas." This saddle contains 166 diamonds, 120 sapphires, 17 rubies, 4 garnets, and 15 pounds of gold and silver. The leather is fully stamped and carved with a profusion of curling vines, flowers, butterflies, and steerheads." This description and a very colorful photograph decorated the cover of S. D. Myres Company catalog many years ago. The worth of this saddle today would be astronomical.

The most colorful mementos of the 101 Ranch Wild West Show, as of any such show, are the posters that were pasted on billboards, fences, sheds, barns, and just about any other place the advance agents could find room for them. They were extremely colorful, highly graphic, and certainly artistic.

Posters of any wild west show are, of course, relatively scarce and those of the 101 Show are no exception. Being pasted to a wall or fence they were hard to retrieve and posters in good condition are extremely rare. The 101 posters that turned a town into an immense picture gallery were made in a variety of sizes, from 28 by 21 inches to 80 by 110 inches. The average poster, however, was 30 by 40 inches.

Programs also were made in all sizes and thicknesses. They consisted of brochures, pamphlets, booklets, and even magazines that contained advertising. These programs contained pictures and stories about the stars and performers travelling with the show and the numerous attractions to be seen.

Programs are more plentiful than posters and, when offered by book stores or so-called "paper parlor" antique stores, are generally less expensive. Their value, as with posters, is established by their age, size, and condition.

Other paper mementos include tickets, passes, route cards, and stationery, all of which were imprinted with Indian head-dresses, bows & arrows, tomahawks, cowboys on bucking horses, all in vivid and lively colors.

No 101 collection can be considered complete without a few of the badges worn by both guards and members of the show. Like everything else connected with this particular show, they were marked with the 101 brand. There are circular German silver badges. One reads — "Guard — 101 Ranch" and another is inscribed "101 Ranch Show — Marland, Okla.-276".

Among the many interesting 101 items is the currency the ranch issued — both in the form of brass tokens and colorful script paper money. A description of one of the paper bills is as follows: the script note measures 7¾ by 3 inches, the face of front of the bill is colored brown, white, and red. The reverse side is green and white, it has the date of 1924 and a serial number #3089. In the center of the front bill is an Indian chief surrounded by stars in a circle. At the top is the name "Miller Brothers 101 Ranch — Round Up Grounds". At the bottom is the State name "Oklahoma" on each side of the circled Indian is marked "5 Bucks" on the left under this is the serial #3089 and the other side is marked "No Cash Value". At the top on each side of the Miller name is the date 1924.

The brass coins are just a barest fraction larger than our half-dollar coin but thinner. The edge of the coin is smooth. The tokens have the value of the coin on one side — 5, 10, 25 cents — with three little stars below the denomination and the name "101 Ranch Store. All three denominations are the same size coin. As of this writing it is unknown if other denominations of coins were ever issued. The above-mentioned coins were very unique, on the opposite side a bas-relief of a cowboy aboard a high flying bucking bronc was depicted. This engraving was made from a photograph of the noted Yakima Canutt, cowboy, winning the Pendleton Roundup of 1912. These bronc tokens were for a time accepted as legal tender by several Oklahoma merchants. In regards to the paper script it was issued in 5, 10, 20 and 50 dollar denominations. The exact uses to which this "money" was put are not known but it is believed it was used by show agents to pay for billboard space, and similar purposes. Those to whom it was given used it to gain admission to the show.

In 1972 something new was added to 101 mementos. A five coin series was created to commemorate the Miller Brothers 101 Ranch and Wild West Show. From 1972 to 1976 a new coin was issued each year. On the first issued coin the likeness of the three Miller Brothers is on one side and on the reverse side the 101 Ranch emblem. The following four coins

Variety of programs from the 101 Show.

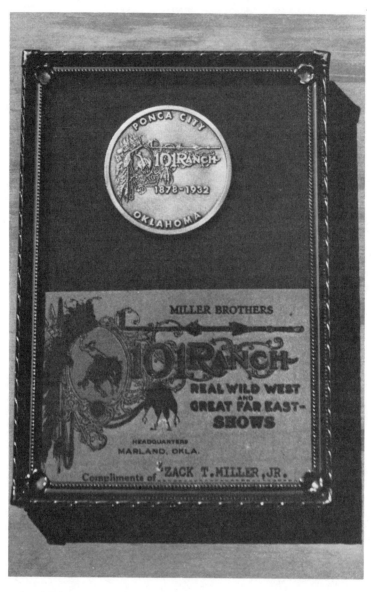

One of the unique solid silver medallions commemorating the 101
Ranch. Series 1972 — Serial No. 81. The medallion was
presented to the author by Zack T. Miller, Jr.

A $10,000 show saddle form the 101 Ranch, Oklahoma.
Woolaroc Museum

Currency used by the 101 Ranch.

A well done display of 101 Ranch wild West memorabilia assembled by Col. Wm. E. Schubert of Pogosa Springs, Colorado, for a 1976 Gun Report show in Milwaukee.

John Battaglia

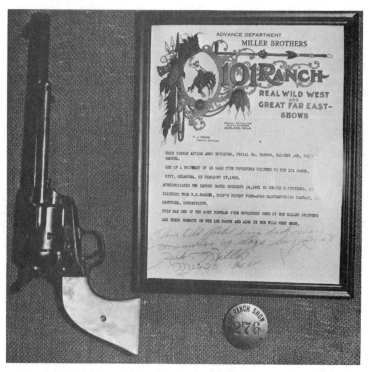

101 marked Colt letter from Zack Miller, Jr. on 101 Ranch
letterhead. The badge was worn by a 101 guard.   *Al Badynski*

each have a scene depicting the 101 Ranch. The coins were minted by the Medallion Art Company of New York City and are struck from .999 silver. There were 500 serialized of silver and 2,500 bronze medallions of the same size. The silver medals sold for $12.50 and the bronze pieces were $3.50 in 1971, just prior to the new coins being available, a second edition of the book "The 101 Ranch" was published. The original was authored in 1937 by Ellsworth Collings and Alma Miller England. The original and the newer books have become important mementos and collector's items. A foreword by the well known Oklahoma author, Glen Shirley, was added to the second issue. This new book was prepared especially for The 101 Ranch Rodeo Foundation, Inc.

Other items connected with the 101 Ranch and Show include postcards and pin buttons. These were sold both at the ranch and by the show in large numbers. Photographs were taken by the thousands and distributed in a variety of sizes. Prints and reprints are not hard to acquire at reasonable prices.

Most interesting and prized of 101 mementos are the firearms used either on the ranch or by members of the show. The most popular handgun with the 101 cowboys, cowgirls, and exhibition shooters was the Colt Single Action Army revolver, mainly in .45 caliber. Colt company records indicate at least 15 single action Colts, and probably many more, were shipped, from time to time, to the 101 Ranch. One occasion according to the records was in February of 1929. Other guns known to have been used during the 101 shows include other model Colts, Smith & Wessons revolvers, Springfield 1873 Model rifles, and Winchester 1892 Saddle Ring carbines in .44-40 caliber, and Colt Lightning carbines.

In the 1960's at Ponca City, Oklahoma, a reunion of 101 oldtimers was sponsored and approximately 30 oldtimers who were associated with the 101 ranch or show attended. Through the years the reunion has continued but its membership has dwindled. It has strived to find a new building to house the many items collected that were once used or related to the 101 Ranch, for future generations to view and enjoy.

To commemorate the reunion of the oldtimers an annual 101 Ranch Rodeo is staged every year in Ponca City. It brings some of the top riders and performers from all over the country. All of this recreates memories of the once famous 101 Ranch, as do the many mementos of the 101.

The 101 Ranch Wild West Show was only one of many such organizations that provided entertainment and excitement for millions of Americans during one of our most colorful eras. Between 1882 and 1946 there were more than a hundred Wild West Shows, any one of which could become the subject of a colorful collection. They were all colorful and each one is a part of our wild west heritage. Preserving the posters, tickets, programs, tokens, and equipment of these shows is a very worthwhile endeavor.

BIBLIOGRAPHY

"101 Ranch" *by Collings/England.*
"The Fabulous Empire" *by Fred Gibson.*
Ponca City News — May 4, 1972.
True West Magazine — July 1971.
Frontier Times Magazine — Summer 1958 — Winter 1958-59.
Tulsa Sunday World — Aug. 25, 1974.
Col. Wm. E. Schubert, Pogosa Springs, Colorado.

CHAPTER VIII

LEGENDARY
POSTER COWBOYS

Who can ever forget his old-time favorite western cinema star? How the hard-riding hero was cheered lustily by multitudes of excited small fry as he and his trusty steed thundered across flickering silver screens in darkened movie houses all over America. If you can't recall a favorite cowboy star, then you've never really known the sheer joy of a Saturday ten-cent matinee.

What drew the boy or girl (mostly boys) into the movie houses were the big colorful posters displayed in the "Coming Attractions" case in front of the neighborhood theaters. These splashy posters depicted the cowboy hero engaged in all manner of thrilling action. Usually they were a collage of full-color illustrations and photographs. Some were real fine works of art.

The titles almost shouted, "Thrills!" "Outlaw Guns," "The Black Voice," "Texas Renegades," "Pioneers of the Frontier," "Outlaw Justice," and countless others. Better to have missed a meal than one of those super attractions. The decision was made right then and there to save every penny so as not to miss a single rip-roarin', action-packed western thriller.

Name your favorite western star and you just about give your age away. Names like Tom Mix, Jack Hoxie, Buck Jones, Tim McCoy, Wild Bill Elliott, Gene Autry, Roy Rogers and Bill Boyd blazoned across the marquee was a guarantee of an exciting two or three hours in a make-believe world. The western wasn't just an exclusive commodity for youngsters; adult fans were just as avid appreciators of blazing six-guns and careening stage-coaches.

Then there were the wonder horses these stars shared billing with, such as Tom Mix's Tony, Jack Hoxie's Scout, Roy Rogers' Trigger and Gene Autry's Champion.

About all you can do today is reminisce about those Saturday afternoon adventures and the daring stars that were our heroes. Gone from the scene are William S. Hart, Tom Mix, Jack Hoxie, Buck Jones, Wild Bill Elliott, among other western cinema pioneers. However, there are still a few of them around, retired, but still remembered.

Gene Autry is a successful businessman. Roy Rogers appears regularly in television specials and at rodeos.

During their screen careers, many Western stars of yesteryear toured between films with circuses, wild west shows and rodeos. This gave fans the opportunity to see and meet their heroes in person. I still thrill to the memory of the many famous Western personalities I had the privilege of meeting and shaking hands with at these shows. I was the envy of every kid for miles around.

Vintage posters that were once plastered all over the entrances and foyers of movie houses are now among the few remaining mementos to remind us of that nostalgic era. And they were sometimes more exciting than the movie itself. A

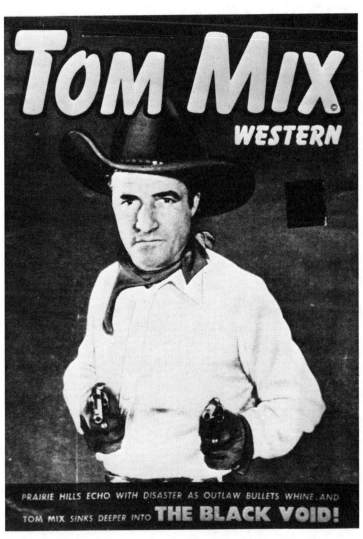

PRAIRIE HILLS ECHO WITH DISASTER AS OUTLAW BULLETS WHINE. AND
TOM MIX SINKS DEEPER INTO **THE BLACK VOID!**

Tom Mix, one of the early and most colorful legendary Western movie heroes ready and rarin' to go with two guns.

Buck Jones, hero of 1930's Westerns. The poster promises plenty of action and thrills.

Tim McCoy, a legend of the movies and wild West shows. His piercing sharp eyes made him a nemesis of lawbreakers. Circa 1930.

"Wild Bill" Elliott a real and "reel" favorite of the matinee Westerns — excitement and fights in every scene. Circa 1930's.

Jack Hoxie who kept the western legends alive in his many exciting movies. Circa 1930's.

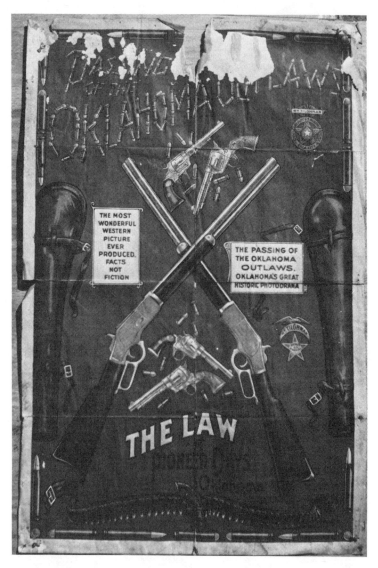

How could the flavor of the old West and shootin' irons be more dramatized than in this colorful and artistic poster? It touts the film, "Passing of the Oklahoma Outlaws", one of the very first produced by a famous lawman of the frontier, Marshall Bill Tilghman. Circa 1900.

good many of the smaller placards that decorated the lobbies are still around. Also available are the 8 x 10 inch glossy prints of the stars and scenes from their movies.

It is the poster that has achieved a prominent place in the wide field of collectables. Once considered as just an inexpensive advertising piece, the poster is now being featured on the walls of art galleries, museums, livingrooms, dens, libraries, and even many restaurants, as well as theater lobbies. The origin of art posters dates back to the 1860's and it was Jules Cheret, the father of lithography, who created the color posters as a popular new art form. Practically every type of art subject and advertising has been introduced in poster form and today it has become a postermania.

Posters come in just about any and every size possible. There are lobby cards 11 x 14 inches and then graduated sizes of ½ sheets, three sheet, six sheet, insert posters, window cards. One western poster collector boasts of a 24-sheet poster.

The majority of movie posters are originally from Cleveland, Ohio, rather than Hollywood, made by the Morgan Lithographing Co., and no doubt others. One of the oldest western movie posters noted by this author is entitled, "Passing of The Oklahoma Outlaws: a movie dramatizing the true story of pioneer days in Oklahoma by the famous frontier Marshal Bill Tilghman. The size is 28 x 42 inches, circa 1900. The litho was made by the Donaldson Litho Co., New Port, Kentucky.

The large posters measure about 41 x 27 inches which makes them difficult to store. Almost every old poster I've come across has been folded. This causes the problem of creases, cracks, or tears in the paper. So the very first thing you must do upon obtaining one of the larger posters is to open it up and place weights on it to flatten it out. Next best thing is to mount it on a heavy mat cardboard obtainable at most any art supply or paint store.

A spray-type rubber cement is very good for mounting your poster to a mat. Cover it with either a clear plastic sheet or a plastic spray. The best procedure, of course, is to put it under glass and frame. Avoid using plastic tape on the face side to repair tears. If you have to use tape, use it on the back. The smaller colored placards and photographs can be placed in plastic sheet covers and stored in albums.

Cost-wise, placards and photographs should run from about twenty-five cents to a dollar apiece. Usually the more you buy, the cheaper they are. Since these smaller items were always more plentiful than the large posters, they have had a far better survival rate.

The price of the large posters depends on many factors, such as condition, age, and the popularity of the Western star. Naturally, the earlier the poster, the more expensive it will be. A poster circa 1920 could cost from $25 on up. Between the 1920's and the 1940's, they become progressively cheaper. The nostalgia craze of recent years and demand for movie posters of all types has pushed prices up. Posters that were selling for five to 25 dollars several years ago could be valued at $100 to $500 and more than $1,000. By the time this book is published it could be even more. The boom is on.

The best source to obtain posters, placards and photos is through the ads in some of the antique trade papers and magazines. You might possibly come across them at flea markets and antique shows. Stores dealing with used books and magazines are another source. None of these items are absolutely scarce, except perhaps the truly *old* ones. Posters dating between the 1940's and 1950's seem to be fairly obtainable. You won't just find them floating around anywhere, though.

Full color reproductions of many old time movie posters, including Westerns, have become available and even miniatures of these are all framed and ready to be hung. Most of the large reproductions are easily identified as such from the originals as the new ones are on heavy stock while the originals are of much lighter paper.

There are only a few museums in the country that contain any sizeable amount of memorabilia to commemorate the old-time western movie stars. Outstanding is the Tom Mix Museum of Dewey, Oklahoma. Another is the William S. Hart Ranch, and also the Park Museum of Newhall, California. Roy Rogers has had the foresight to preserve his many mementoes in a museum at Apple Valley, California.

One of the largest western movie poster collections known to this author belongs to Don Look of Colorado who is credited of having more than 10,000 posters. Stories of this most impressive collection have appeared in Argosy Magazine, the Denver Post's Empire Magazine, and the American Collector Magazine, November, 1978, issue.

BIBLIOGRAPHY

The American Collector — *November 1978.*
Chicago Tribune Tempo Section — *Movie Posters* — *Aug. 11, 1979.*

CHAPTER IX

THE LORE OF THE BULLWHIP

Crack the whip — graceful or deadly — it can be either if manipulated by an experienced man. If you have ever seen a whip artist perform at a circus, a rodeo, or in the movies, in his hands a whip comes alive. Black and supple, it can strike with all the sudden deadliness of a snake. With a snap and crack the whip artist can encircle the waist or ankle of his assistant, or he can cut paper from an assistant's hand, or a cigarette from the mouth. Unlike a bullet, the whip has an uncanny way for its target.

It's true that the whipping post, the slave, the buggy, have disappeared from the American scene. So it would seem that the bullwhip would go the same way. But the truth of the matter is, the bullwhip is as popular as ever.

Who buys them? Many are still sold to men who work with cattle, horses, and other animals. The drover's whip is much in use around large stockyards. Of course the animal trainer could not possibly be without one, and large, professional-type whips are used in the training of Artic dog sled teams, and for training dogs in military and police work. "Bullwhip Manipulator" is the title used by the whip artists who demonstrate their dexterity with uncanny skill, and many whips are purchased by performers, both amateurs and professional.

Who makes these whips? There are several leather companies who include whips, along with their other leather products such as holsters, belts, and miscellaneous leather items. Back in the 1960's the leather firm of J. M. Bucheimer of West Virginia is reputed to have turned out more than 1,500 whips a month. They produced an assortment of whips from short riding quirts to the fifty foot whips favored by circus ringmasters. The usual run is six to twenty feet long. A skilled, fast leather worker can produce one whip every hour and ten minutes. Cowhide is used most commonly, but pliable kangaroo hide is also a popular material.

An important part of the whip is the cracker, which is the tip. This is the popper or noisy end, and is usually made of dental floss or nylon. It attains the speed of a bullet when it is cracked. In the hands of a professional, the bullwhip is as dangerous a weapon as you could find, and the popper, when snapped, is sharp as a razor blade. Some of the feats performed are astounding.

Through the years there have been many professional, skilled bullwhip manipulators who performed in the circus, Wild West shows, and of course the movies. There have been several western movie stars who specialized in demonstrating their skills with the whip in many of their exciting matinee movies, including Lash LaRue and Whip Wilson, their nicknames certainly related to their use of whips. A real great of the old Western movies was Colonel Tim McCoy who not only was fast on the draw with his trusty six-shooter but who was also an expert in the use of a bullwhip. He was in his 70's and even 80's touring the country with a wild west show and giving exhibitions of his skill with bullwhips.

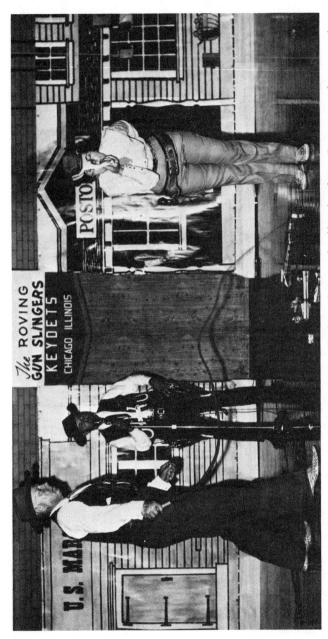

Whip artist Chuck Monell cuts a flaming paper tube from the mouth of his daughter, Corinne, in his act with the Roving Gunslinger Wild West Show. Announcer in the background is Author George Virgines, then a deputy marshal of Dodge City.

Whip Wilson, a favorite Western movie matinee hero cracking a whip as he pursued the "bad guys" on horseback.

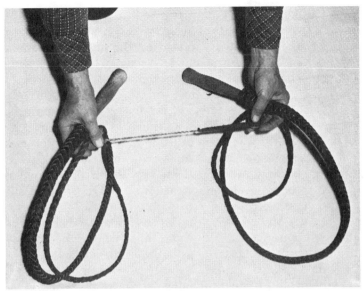

The "popper" at the end of a bullwhip is shown. Usually made of dental floss of nylon, the "popper" attains the speed of a bullet and can cut like a razor blade.

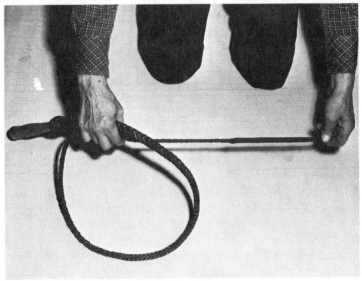

A leather thong at the end of a bullwhip.

115

Lash LaRue, another cowboy movie star of the 1940's and 50's, used his whip and gun to straighten out the outlaws. He later became an evangelist in Florida and the mission features a Hollywood Western Revue in which some of Lash LaRue's old gun and whip trick movies are featured.

The western movie hero, Whip Wilson, is another star who demonstrated his ambidextrous use of a bullwhip in the movies. He carried his whip in a special holder on the left side of his gun belt. If the script called for a gun to be whiplashed out of a desperado's hand, Whip was the man who could do it, even on horseback. Whip Wilson, with his bullwhip, has proven to be a novel Saturday matinee idol for many young and old fans alike.

Chuck Monell was a whip artist who, as a member of the Roving Gunslinger's Wild West Show, toured the country demonstrating his dexterity as bullwhip manipulator. Assisting him was his daughter, Corinne, who was a former rodeo trick rider. Chuck could cut a sheet of paper, which he had his daughter hold for him, in half, quarters, and smaller. Another trick is cutting the tip of a rolled piece of paper until there is only an inch or so left. His daughter had the ticklish task of holding a flaming tube of paper in her mouth while her confident dad cuts the blazing end off with an eight-foot bullwhip. Another unique feat by Chuck was to take a fourteen foot bullwhip and execute a wrap-around trick with his famed horse, Flyer, who was also known as the "Fire Jumping Horse". This was a very difficult trick to perform. Chuck wrapped the whip around the horse's hind leg, around the belly, front legs and neck. Both Chuck and Flyer had to spend many hours perfecting this unique act and feat.

An old time, but famous, bullwhip artist is Dave Kashner, who was known as "the man who whips the stars". For forty years or more Dave has been the man who tortured the screen heroes. He is the movie companies' recognized whip expert. Movie and television directors would call upon Kashner whenever they needed someone to administer a savage lashing to a screen character. In 1922 Douglas Fairbanks, Sr., hired Dave as a trainer and he worked in Hollywood ever since, having worked in more than 500 movies. One question asked is how he raises the realistic welts that would appear on a star's body each time the whip lands. To this Kashner would reply, "It's easy. I simply soak the whip in a pot of red ink so it works like a rubber stamp."

Anyone attempting to duplicate any of the aforementioned whip tricks should remember to use common sense, and safety is the first essential. With some discretion, becoming adept with a whip, like countless other sports such as archery, horseback riding, or fast draw with a gun, can be a source of joy and accomplishment. But before you try to copy the artistry of a professional bullwhip manipulator, a word of advice, these stunts are not for the beginner. There are plenty of simple tricks, however, that can be mastered without danger.

So crack the whip! Live by the lash! You, too, can become a member of the great fraternity of bullwhippers.

BIBLIOGRAPHY

J. M. Bucheimer Leather Co., Cameron, W. VA.

CHAPTER X

WAGON WHEELS
KEEP ROLLIN'

There was a time when the turning of wagon wheels meant the expansion and settling of our country. Covered wagons transported the pioneers to new frontiers; stagecoaches hauled passengers and valuables to the new settlements; supplies and provisions had to be delivered to remote townsites. Ore and other commodities had to be hauled to mills and processing plants; produce had to be transported to market. And the familiar buckboard was used by farmers and ranchers to pick up their daily necessities.

Perhaps the wheels that supported the most publicized and famous vehicle of the Old West is the stagecoach. Scattered throughout the country are numerous museums, historical societies, restored pioneer and western towns that feature these majestic coaches of history.

Abbot and Downey & Company of Concord, New Hampshire, pioneer maker of the stagecoach, manufactured at least 3,000 coaches with the famous name "Concord Coach". Volumes have been written about these unique and history-making coaches and the many stage lines that used them, especially throughout the West. Of course Wells, Fargo & Co. is perhaps the most noted and famous name related to the stagecoach.

The construction and history of these coaches is a story in itself, so for the sake of this wagon wheel story we'll concentrate on stagecoach wheels. All of the wheels used on the various wagons and coaches built by Abbot & Downey were of the same dimensions; this was for the heavy and light coaches, mud wagons, and passenger hacks. The front wheels had 12 spokes, tire widths varied between 2½ and 3 inches, and were 46 inches in diameter; the rear wheels had 14 spokes and were 61 inches in diameter. Color of the wheels were lemon yellow with black striping which contrasted greatly with the striking red body.

One of the oldest companies to make wagon wheels was the Hoopes Brothers and Darlington, Inc. of Westchester, Pennsylvania. They were established in 1866 and were still in business into the late 1960's.

In the beginning they only made spokes for other wheelwrights, but by the 1870's they were making wagon wheels and even exporting them to the Emperor of France for his fancy coach. The covered wagons that rolled westward after the Civil War and during the Spanish American War all probably had wheels that were made by Hoopes Bros. & Darlington, Inc. After the turn of the century when automobiles began to crowd the roads the company turned to making more than 100,000 wooden automobile wheels.

Studebaker is definitely a name that is synonymous with wagons. It began as a small business in South Bend, Indiana, in 1852 and it grew to a giant factory of 100 acres, 4,000 workers, 60,000,000 feet of lumber in seasoning sheds, plus, 500,000 hubs for wheels. Their slogan was — "One Every

Seven Minutes." They built just about every type wagon imaginable — chuck wagons, ammunition and transport wagons, ambulances, artillery caissons, carts for hauling beer; school buses, coal and lumber wagons, and of course the farmer's utility Studebaker wagon. This wagon compared to what the pickup truck is today. It was the farmer's favorite and it was a common sight to see a line of Studebaker wagons with their green painted bodies and red trim, and red wheels in town on a weekend.

Although many varieties of vehicles are preserved in museums and private collections throughout the country, their wheels — in various states of repair — decorate driveways in suburbs, and on farms and ranches. Perhaps more wagon wheels have been preserved than any other western item. People from coast to coast and border to border enjoy displaying this relic.

The wagon, like today's automobile, supported many fringe industries. A wheelwright, whose trade it was to make and repair wagon wheels, was part of every town's business section. A wheelwright's shop would consist of carpenters, blacksmith, mechanic, and painters, depending on its size. The wheelwright had no machinery as we know it today. Every wheel had to be built and fashioned by hand with chisels, planes, saws, shaves, adzes and perhaps a lathe and bandsaw. But as time went on they replaced their primitive machinery with more efficient types.

All of the lumber used for wheels had to be properly seasoned. After the logs — oak, ash or elm — were brought to the wheelwright's shop they were cut into rough lengths for the spokes, felloes and hubs, then stored and allowed to season. Each piece of lumber used for the felloes and spokes had to be knot free and seasoned just right. The wheelwright went through a careful series of hewing and shaping, then fitting the spokes to the felloes and stock or hub. This was followed by the "ringing" of the wheel (fitting the iron tire). The wheel had to have a definite dish to it for maximum strength so that the load-bearing spoke, as the wheel revolved, was always perpendicular to the ground.

Sizes of wheels vary greatly. Some wheels, such as those

used in the lumber industry in the early days, reached a height of nine feet. An excellent example of these is on exhibit in Clinch Park, Traverse City, Michigan. Back in 1932 this giant set of nine-foot logging wheels was procured by Harold Titus from the Antrim Iron Company of Michigan. They were drawn in the annual National Cherry Festival parade at that time and since have attracted the attention of thousands of tourists. They now stand as a monument to the passing of a great lumber era.

The normal size of wheels used on passenger hacks, heavy coaches, light coaches, and mud wagons were a standard 46inches in diameter for the front wheel and 61" diameter for the rear. Tire widths could be anything from about two to three inches, and sometimes wider depending on the vehicle.

One of the legendary freighters of the West was California's 20 mule team, this was the noted Borax team and wagon. They consisted of ten-spans, eighteen mules and two heavy horses in the wheel position. The outfit comprised a water wagon, and two borax wagons and the length of all this was 150 feet. The front wheels were five feet high and the rear wheels were seven feet high, all with iron tires eight inches wide and one inch thick.

Color schemes for wheels were somewhat standard. Stagecoaches had bright yellow; funeral carriages naturally were black; work or express wagons were either red or green. But many people preferred the natural varnish finish and others chose gaudier or personal colors.

Perhaps the most glamorous and colorful wheel was the circus wheel. When the circus came to town it paraded its ornate wagons through the streets to advertise its performances. The wagons traveled at the speed of a walking horse (about three and one-half miles an hour), just fast enough to cause the bright paint on the wagon wheels to spin in animated designs.

The circus wheel was massive. Circus wagons had to move daily regardless of conditions or weather. When a wagon bogged down in sand or mud the drivers kept adding horses (or sometimes elephants) until the wagon literally was dragged

Wagon wheel flower trellis.

Patio table made from an old wagon wheel with welded chain legs and horseshoe feet.

Wagon wheel gate ready to be installed with horseshoe latch.

Wagon wheel hub lamp.

125

"End of the Line". This painting by talented artist W. T. Zivic of
Arizona, depicted the fate of many stagecoaches.

These old wagon wheels have finally stopped rollin'.

Author George Virgines, as a member of the Roving Gunslinger's Wild West Show, holds up a stagecoach. This is a replica coach.

A massive colorful wagon wheel from circus wagon days.
Circus World Museum, Baraboo, Wisconsin

out of the mire. The wheels just had to hold up.

The St. Mary's Wheel & Spoke Company of St. Mary's, Ohio, made the majority of the heavy circus-style wheels during the first three decades of this century. The heaviest wheels weighed about 450 pounds, were eight inches wide, and ringed by a steel tire that was one inch thick. The diameter of these wheels ranged from 30 inches to 52 inches.

Today one can see colorful circus wheels at the Circus World Museum in Baraboo, Wisconsin. Here they restore and rebuild all types of circus parade wagons. According to Museum Director Charles (Chappie) Fox, "No imagination on our part is incorporated into any of the wagons." Every vehicle they obtain is seriously researched so that it can be authentically restored to its actual construction and colors, including the wheels.

In this mechanized age the wagon wheel has just about slipped into oblivion. However just because the wheel is no longer on a wagon or carriage it still can be useful. Rather than relegate these old and sometimes historic wheels to the junk yard, all you have to do is tour the countryside to see the many useful and decorative ways they have been put to use. One farmer in Nebraska used 220 wheels to make a fence, an eye stopper to say the least.

Beside gracing the entrances to driveways, the wagon wheel can be used as an antique trellis alongside a lamp-post; made into fences; or used in unusual window modeling. Or it can hold up a mailbox, be used as a patio table or a garden gate. Another novel use is to put a pair together like a small ferris wheel and use them as a holder for pots of flowers.

They also lend a Western touch to rustic indoor decoration. Perhaps the most common and popular item is the wagon wheel chandelier with several lanterns attached. A most useful addition to a den or family room is a coffee table fashioned from an old wheel with welded chain links or horse hames for legs, and a glass top. The large hub makes an excellent base for a lamp. The possibilities are as endless as your imagination.

Where are these relics of the old wagon days obtainable and how much do they cost? Your local farmer or rancher is a good source. I have obtained the wheels I own at a nominal price (from about $1.00 to perhaps $3.00 or $4.00). Old junk shops are another good source. The cost, depending on the size and condition, can range from a couple of dollars to as much as ten. The supply, however, is not unlimited and their cost probably will increase as the number available dwindles.

BIBLIOGRAPHY

Wells Fargo History Room, Wells Fargo Bank, San Francisco, CA.

Circus World Museum, Baraboo, Wisconsin.

Traverse City Area Chamber of Commerce, Traverse City, Mich.

"The Wheelwrights Shop" *by George Sturt.*

The Southwesterner — Apr. 1963 — "Abbot-Downey Co. — Makers of the Historic Concord Coach" *by Carl J. Bell.*

Old West — Summer 1968 — "Wagons By Studebaker" *by Anthony A. Amaral.*

CHAPTER XI

HORSESHOE LORE

Next time you happen to find an old, rusty horseshoe, don't throw the thing over your left shoulder for good luck. Hang onto it instead. It could well be the seedling of a new and interesting hobby. The history of horseshoes goes back quite a few centuries — equipping horses with iron shoes precedes by far the era "when Knighthood was in flower." At one time in England, horseshoes and horseshoe nails were actually used as money. Rents and taxes were paid in such manner and this could be where the term, "hard cash" originated.

In the early days of chariot racing it was common practice to protect the hoofs of prize horses with socks or sandals. They used iron-solded leather socks called "soleae."

But this idea eventually gave way to something more substantial and lasting. Iron itself came to be utilized for making horseshoes more durable. This practice was noted at the time of the Roman Empire when its Legions were endeavoring to conquer the ancient world.

The brass seal of Ralph of Norman Times, (he was the farrier of the Norman-French Bishorpric of Durham) had such symbols. A silver Greek coin from 300 BC depicts a person possibly working on the hoof of a horse. The town of Gloucester, England, of the 1300's had part of its seal decorated with horseshoes and related implements. In the 9th century the Emperor Leo VI listed in a record that crescent shaped iron horseshoes and nails were used for the cavalry's equipment. This suggests that the "Village Blacksmith" of earlier days was an important personage. As evidenced in early illustration, horses were large and were shod with many types of heavy shoes. Consequently, blacksmiths had to be strong — another factor which contributed to their community stature.

Emperors and noblemen had to show off their wealth and power. This they did by having their favorite animals attired in gold or silver shoes. As may be imagined, these were sought-after items and real lucky pieces to the finders. You may be sure they didn't throw that precious metal over their shoulders!

Since the Spanish *Conquistadors* introduced horses into the New World, the size and shape of horseshoes have changed very little. The material from which they were made and the different tasks which called for particular type shoes have been the only variants. As our frontier pushed West, horses played an all important role. Seemingly endless streams of wagontrains creaked their way westward, many teamsters driving oxen and mules heavily shod with iron, as were the horses. Stagecoaches hauled the mail, passengers, and the valuable gold and silver shipments. Ore, farm, and merchant wagons were needed to transport commodities necessary to a way of life. There were fancy carriages, buckboards, and the horse remudas of the cattle ranches. All contributed to the ever-increasing horse population.

The need for a variety of breeds for the many specialized

tasks encountered in the cities, on farms, and ranches — not to forget the U. S. Cavalry — necessitated a corresponding variety of horseshoes. Special shoes to meet any type of condition and terrain also had to be devised. A good blacksmith was a real technician. For the load-pulling horse he made sturdy, heavy shoes; for the milk or bread wagon horses, a "quiet" type shoe was needed. This was accomplished with rubber and cork. For the horse with a bad hoof, a shoe with a bar across it to hold the hoof together, was used. Ice shoes were equipped with sharp points to enable a horse to negotiate icy or slippery roads and streets. Then there are several types of shoes for thoroughbred race horses. With pony shoes, mule and oxen shoes, you have an interesting assortment from which to choose.

In 1871 New York City had 1,600 horses in one car barn for use on the horsecar lines. Before the advent of the horseless carriage, cities depended on the horse for pulling street cars and carriage cabs, while heavy draft horses were used to pull the commercial wagons of business houses. Then there were the mounted policemen and the privately maintained stables. All this added up to a large concentration of horses in the more populated cities and towns.

Though it's a long cry since medieval times, the horseshoe is still very much in evidence in this modern space age. Proof of this is in the fact that manufacturers in the United States presently list over 300 styles and a varied range of weights, with an output of 8 million horseshoes per year. Modern horseshoes are shipped in metal half-keg containers. They used to be shipped in wooden kegs. Modern ones are of special drop-forged steel, well balanced and accurately shaped, designed for long wear. They come as common horseshoes, driving and draft shoes. Their weights vary from 8¾-oz. aluminum shoes to 40-oz. steel models. So all and all, you can't classify the horseshoe as merely an item of the past, or scarce.

The antiquarian-type collector might consider, for example, horseshoes which trace the evolution of shoes, and strive to round out a collection which would represent a broad scope of history.

Perhaps an easier collection to assemble would be the many types of horseshoes worn for specialized jobs or worn by various domestic breeds. This would include draft horses, race horses, cow-ponies, show horses, pack animals and many more.

The diverse sized and shaped shoes can be enjoyed simply as decorative pieces, or turned into usable accessories. I'll have to admit that it has been this latter category which most appealed to me. The many useful and decorative items that can be made from horse and pony shoes is limited only by individual imagination. Nothing sets off Western decor or complements it more dramatically than these lucky old shoes converted to play a practical role in our present-day life. Starting with the outdoors — in the yard, barn, corral, and tack house — gate latches and hinges, fence rails set to fit into horseshoes placed on poles, boot scrapers, door knockers, garden bells, hooks, dinner gongs, signs, and flower pot holders are but a few examples of adaptation.

In the house, the lowly horseshoe may appear non-descript in comparison with beautifully crafted items such as firearms, lawmen's badges, Bowie knives, spoons, dishes or coins, but none-the-less, a unique item of horse footgear can be fashioned into electric or candle sconces, candle holders.

Just about any type of furniture can be created out of horseshoes for patio or lawn — rockers, chairs, lounges, tables, and magazine racks.

One other use for a horseshoe (not too practical, though) — an old range country recipe for good coffee calls for boiling the coffee until it will float a horseshoe — just let the imagination run rampant.

The game of horseshoes dates back as far as the Middle Ages, 500 AD to 1450 AD when soldiers began using discarded shoes for tossing and it later became an army game. With Romans invading England they also carried the idea of this game and gradually the aristocracy adopted it as a favorite pastime. England in turn introduced horseshoes to the American colonials and later the game advanced with the westward settling of the United States. It was in 190 when the first horseshoe club was organized.

For those who are not very handy with tools, they are

A unique and functional horseshoe table adorned with two candlesticks made from pony shoes.

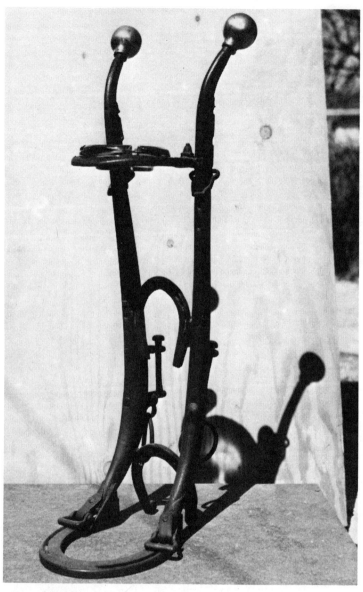

Four horseshoes, a pair of hames and an ashtray become a decorative and useful smoking stand at the hands of a clever artisan.

Many sizes and shapes of horseshoes are displayed on a board. The large heavy shoes might have been used for a big and powerful draft horse while the small and dainty irons likely went to shoe a pony.

Horseshoe relics adorn a display board. Top, left to right: Shoe found in Columbus, New Mexico. Two shoes from the famous old 101 Ranch in Ponca City, Oklahoma. A very old rusty shoe found in Billy the Kid country, Lincoln County, New Mexico. Bottom, left to right: Two miniature shoes made by a blacksmith at Henry Ford's Greenfield Village Museum near Detroit, Michigan. An old mule shoe found in a mine at Kingman, Arizona.

A variety of useful and decorative items made from horseshoes. Upper Row, left to right: A pair of shoes and a Mexican spur make a bookend. A good luck trivet. A souvenir copper shoe with Arizona inscribed on it. A horseshoe becomes a coat hook. Two shoes go to make a rifle hook. Bottom, left to right: A pong shoe has been formed to make a cabinet handle. Another shoe forms an ashtray. Yet another innovative use is for a door knocker and last, a pony shoe has been made into a candlestick.

many stores, gift shops, junk and antique shops, and mail order houses which sell these unusual and decorative horseshoe articles.

There is one other intriguing aspect to collecting horseshoes. In old towns, backwoods, farmsites and ranches that I have had the good fortune and permission to prospect, I've come upon many an old rusty horseshoe, mule and pony shoe, and on occasion, an oxen shoe. These particular finds — nostalgic relics of days gone by — have become real mementoes of the trips. In poking around the famous Miller Brothers' former 101 Ranch in Oklahoma I found three old rusty horseshoes which are certainly historical relics of significance and a great remembrance of that particular trip. While in Lincoln County, New Mexico, I dug up a battered horseshoe which brought to mind Bill the Kid days. Other shoes — relics of the old frontier — that I have been fortunate in finding are from Columbus, New Mexico, dating back to Pancho Villa's raid; a mule shoe from an old mine in Kingman, Arizona; and a pony shoe from Buffalo Bill's Wild West Show. Old, rusty, and dilapidated, they with the rest of my collection represent fond memories of some particular part of the past which I cherish.

This is probably the cheapest way of collecting horseshoes and souvenirs from trip or vacation, but it's not always the easiest method. It means a lot of prospecting, asking questions, crawling and getting into the most unusual places, and perhaps a little manual labor too. But if you ever find any horseshoes this way, you'll never forget it.

Of course, you can't always be lucky enough to find one everywhere you travel, so the alternative is to pay cash. You can almost be sure of finding horseshoes in any old junk shop at a cost of a dollar — most times less.

For those who would prefer a nice, clean, shiny replica for a souvenir, these can be bought at most souvenir shops. They might not be real horseshoes, but they have the same design and usually bear the name of the town or state in which you secure them.

The far-sighted collector will realize that the distinctive novelties of today are the rarities of tomorrow.

142

At historical villages, and some museums in various parts of the country, authentic miniature horseshoes can be purchased which have been forged by blacksmiths operating replica shops. Displays of horseshoe collections are also frequently exhibited at pioneer villages and historical societies. It might be worthwhile to check into those in your area.

There are many superstitions and curious beliefs associated with the horseshoe and fitting the exact age or origin to these fancies is difficult to say the least. Even on some of the old sailing ships horseshoes have been noted to be nailed to the mast. A good example was the famous seaman Lord Nelson of England who is said to have nailed a horseshoe to the mast of his ship the HMS Victory, in the battle of Trafalgar.

In certain parts of Pennsylvania they hang their horseshoes with the heels downward "so the luck will be spilled into the house." The custom in Germany was to hang the horseshoe with the heels pointing upward as a protection against all sorts of vile things such as "lightning, fire, fiends, and hags." Throughout Europe, Asia, and America, wherever there are horses, the lucky horseshoe is sure to be displayed. In the noted "Believe It Or Not" by Ripley series, it was stated that the door of St. Nickolas Church in Steinbuhl, Germany, is covered with horseshoes to assure good health for the animals that wore them.

As a last suggestion concerning equine footgear; make sure you hang your horseshoe over the door with the open end up. That way, your luck will never pour or spill out. Matter of fact, your luck might just turn out to be so good you'll stumble upon a *real silver* horseshoe in an old *Conquistador* hangout somewhere along Southwestern trails. That's not so wild a dream, either!

BIBLIOGRAPHY

Diamond Calk Horseshoe Co., Duluth, Minn.
"Horseshoe Sculptures" *by Roger Buchanan.*
"Believe It Or Not" *by Ripley.*
The Western Horseman Magazines — May, 1961 — June, 1962 — June, 1968 — Sept., 1970-Oct. 1972.

CHAPTER XII

TELLTALE MARKS

If this gun could only talk!" is a dream-wish known to every collector. But all that most guns commonly say is "Bang!" when you pull the trigger.

Yet some guns bear symbols and markings that do talk, after a fashion, if you have the patience for the research necessary to interpret the message. You find the marks on various parts of the gun — barrel or backstrap, frame or grips; the information from which the interpretation can be drawn comes, if at all, from the most unexpected sources!

Certainly one of the most talked about, most written about, of all revolvers — of all guns, for that matter — is "the gun that helped win the West," "the Peacemaker," the Colt Single Action Army revolver, prosaically labeled at the Colt factory "the Model P." So much sheer romance surrounds the Colt Single Action in all of its stages of development that it stands almost unchallenged as the symbol of the American West. Much of that romance is fiction, but much of it is history. It is difficult, sometimes, to separate the one from the other. But the markings can help.

The many "standard" Colt markings are more or less self-explanatory; or, if not self-explanatory, explained by the meticulous studies that have been made and published. Every variation in the spelling, style of lettering, and location on the gun of the Colt name, address, patent inscription, and caliber markings had, or has been given, meaning. These can and usually do tell you when, where, and for what market the gun was built. Among the significant barrel markings are the model name designations: "Colt Single Action Army," "Bisley Model," and "Colt Frontier Six-Shooter,' followed by caliber markings. The caliber markings alone can be revealing and sometimes add to a gun's value.

But to me, the special markings are the ones that have won my deepest interest and cost me time and money in research. Some of that research has been frustrating, but most has been rewarding.

Among the special markings I refer to are those stamped on by the Colt factory for large purchasers. One such customer was Wells Fargo & Company. Guns made for Wells Fargo had the initials 'W. F. & Co." stamped on the flat of the butt. And those initials alone are enough to surround the gun with an aura of adventure and excitement for every student of the West.

Wells Fargo Colts can be authenticated, within limits, by the relationship between the stamped initials and other markings. They were ordered by the Wells Fargo purchasing office in New York, and redistributed from there. Some Wells Fargo Colts have been found which bear serial numbers in the range of 137,000. These could have been made about 1891. Most of the Wells Fargo guns carry serial numbers of from 308,000 to around 311,000.

However, in checking the Colt Company records I found some orders from the Wells Fargo Company which place some

Single Action's in the 288,000 range. Apparently they were never purchased in large, single orders, but in lots of from 4 to 8 at one time, which would scatter the serial number range. A truly authenticated W. F. & Co. Colt is indeed a historic weapon with a story behind it.

Other special factory marked Single Actions that inspire interest and have turned up from time to time carry the markings, "E. de Mex," for the Government of Mexico, and "G. M. Parral," for the Chihuahua Mine. The San Antonio Police Department used the Colt SA in quantity up to 1927. They are supposed to be one of the last police departments to order the SA's. Their guns were marked "S.A.P.D." on the butt strap.

Another Colt with an intriguing marking is a SA, Serial No. 143990, caliber .44-40. Stamped on the left side of the barrel is the name. "Mexican National R.R.". According to the Colt records, twelve guns with this marking were shipped on January 12, 1892, with 7½ inch barrels. Holsters and belts were furnished with the revolvers. This old railroad is now operating under the name, National Railways of Mexico. A stimulating question comes to the mind of the romanticist: "How many gold shipments were guarded on the train with this gun?"

Our "south of the border" neighbor, Mexico, is also represented with another Model P which started out as a "Mexican Mystery Colt." It was just a standard Colt SA, Serial No. 39707, caliber .45. But stamped on the barrel over the standard Colt address marking were the letters "R M" and a sunburst pattern. The letters "R M" were also stamped on the side of the cylinder.

With the generous assistance of fellow collectors, this marking was determined to be of Mexican origin. The "R M" denotes "Republica de Mexicana," and the sunburst symbol is found on the Mexican peso. According to Colt records, 400 guns of this type were shipped July 22, 1879, to the Wexel & DeGress Company of New York and Mexico City. The size of the order would suggest a government purchase, and such "R M" markings have been found on Mexican Government property of various periods.

147

The era in which these markings were used is the period in Mexican history that parallels the years in our own West when the gun was the law of the land. Eighteen seventy-six was the year of revolt in Mexico, when the General Porfirio Diaz became President. A part of General Diaz' force were the Mexican Rurales. They were mounted police, magnificent horsemen, and picked sharpshooters. The Colt Single Action Army revolver was very much a part of their equipment.

A "US" marked Colt SA is not unusual, but it represents a very significant era in the history of the U. S. Army and of our country. It brings to mind such names as General George A. Custer, the 7th Cavalry, the Little Big Horn, the Indian Wars, and the settling of the northwestern and southwestern territories. Any Colt SA bearing authentic "US" marking is almost definitely a relic of our Western heritage.

One Colt SAA which is not unusually marked is interesting because the address on the top of the barrel shows how widespread the popularity of the model really was. This SA was an English address, "Colt's PT-FA Mfg. Co. Hartford, CT. U.S.A. Depot 14 Pall Mall, London." Pistols with this marking were exported to England, and the permission for this stamping was granted by the Commissioners of Her Magesty's Customs in 1876. One SA so marked is in .455 Eley caliber, Serial No. 98033, with British proof marks. According to Colt records, this gun was shipped with 87 others in 1883 to the Colt London Agency, London, England. The history of this particular weapon demonstrates that the "Wild West" did not have sole priority on the Colt SA. A British Officer bought the gun in England and carried it as his personal side arm in India during the 1st World War. Then, as a retired officer in Nairobi, Kenya, Africa, in order to supplement a meager retirement pay, he finally sold the gun to a district health officer of the British Government who was also a gun collector. But, due to the uprising of terrorists in Africa, he was advised to rid himself of his collection lest they fall in the wrong hands. The gun in question returned to America, thus completing a 77-year cycle of war and adventure to end up where it started.

After "the winning of the West" was accomplished,

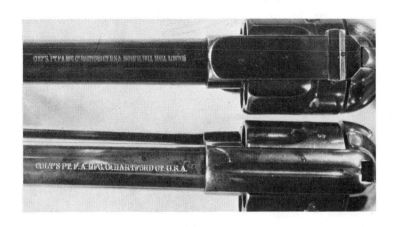

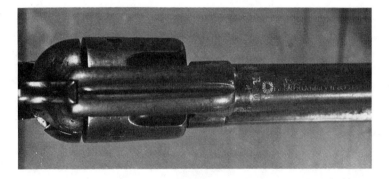

Barrel markings on Colt revolvers provide information about the weapons. Upper: Top barrel marking is Colt's London address and below it the standard address mark for the United States. Lower: This barrel marking on a Colt SAA includes an "R M" and sunburst design. The "R M" denotes "Republica de Mexicana" and the sunburst is found on Mexico's peso coin.

Upper: This deeply engraved "101 Ranch" marking on the butt of a Colt SAA represents the famous ranch. Lower: The marks "E. de Mex" on the barrel of this Colt SAA .38-40 caliber show it is related to the government of Mexico.

The special markings on the side of the barrel of this weapon, "125th ANNIVERSARY — SAA MODEL .45 CAL.", denotes the Colt Firearms Company anniversary in 1961. This handsome gun had a royal blue finish and was trimmed in gold plate.

something new was added to the American scene in the birth of the Wild West Show. The Wild West Show was the predecessor of the Western movies and finally of our "adult" television westerns. Nothing did more to immortalize and glamorize "the gun that helped win the West," the Colt Single Action Army revolver.

One model that was used as a prop in a Wild West Show is a Colt SA, caliber .45, Serial No. 353046. On the right side of the frame in crude stamping are the numerals "101." The Colt records revealed that 15 guns of the same type were shipped on February 27, 1929, to the 101 Ranch, of Ponca City, Oklahoma. That crude 101 stamping represents one of the West's famous brands and one of the most famous Wild West Shows in history, the Miller Brothers 101 Ranch Wild West Show.

Since the discovery of this "101" Colt many other guns related to this famous ranch and wild West show have come to light. Many of these firearms, either plain or fancy engraved, representing some famous personage or owner of the ranch, have such markings to relate them to the "101".

This famous ranch show toured England in the early 1900's, and later was revived in 1925, to last until 1931. Such famous personages as Tom Mix, Buck Jones, Jack Hoxie, Buffalo Bill, Will Rogers, and many others, appeared with this show at one time or another. And so what started out as an ordinary Colt with a crude marking led to a study of a world-renowned Wild West Show and another important phase of American history.

Unusual markings are intriguing and challenging. Such is the case with the Colt SAA, Serial No. 124626, caliber .44-40. Records of the Colt factory state that this particular gun left the factory on Dec. 22, 1887, in a shipment of 19 guns sold to the Schoverling, Daly, & Gales Co. of New York, N.Y. What represents a real challenge is the marking, letters "A MM CO." stamped on the right side of the frame. Here is a mystery-marked Colt that has seen much use from its appearance. The clues to its background are meager. It was recently found in California. Where, when, and how nobody knows, as yet. But its California origin, and with the letters A

152

MM CO. might suggest a mining company, since the state of California is considered the "Mother Lode" country. Some mining companies with initials that coincide with the markings are the American Mining & Mineral Supply Co.; the Amalgamated Mining & Mineral Co. of San Francisco in the 1880's; Acme Miners & Mining Supply Co., also of San Francisco, circa 1870 to the 1890's.

These are just early names, and it may be that the gun is not connected with the mining industry at all. But to make this mystery a bit more challenging, just recently several Webley Mark IV revolvers turned up with the A MM CO. markings on the backstrap, along with such additional markings as "B D E," and "R H A." Could this give the "A MM CO." Colt a British connection? For now, it remains a challenge, a mystery with no solution.

As the popularity of the Colt Single Action continues as a collector's item, more unusually marked Colts are being discovered. In the past few years such telltale marks have been noted, although not completely verified. These include "U.S.I.S." for United States Indian Service and "U.S.I.D." for United States Interior Department (this has not been proven to be conclusive).

Not too many years ago an interesting marking "W.C.C." was discovered on a Colt SAA and some time was involved before discovering that it was a property mark showing that the gun belonged to the "Western Costume Company", a California company that rents props and costumes to the movies. Another Colt SAA, caliber .45, serial number 141687 had the butt marked "MO. PAC. RY." which stands for the Missouri Pacific Railroad Company. This particular Colt was shipped to the E. C. Meacheam Co. of St. Louis, Missouri, in July of 1891. It so happens that this railroad company had a large office located there.

Every Colt SAA has a story. It might be the caliber, the barrel length, the presentation or engraved model, or just a few letters or numerals crudely stamped somewhere on the revolver. There are approximately 357,859 stories the Colt SAA's could tell, since that is about the number of Colt SAA's that were manufactured between 1873 to 1941. Which of these stories could your gun tell — if it could talk?

BIBLIOGRAPHY

"Peacemaker and Its Rivals" *by John E. Parsons.*

"Colt Firearms" *by James E. Serven.*

"The Colt Revolver" *by Charles T. Haven & Frank A. Belden.*

Jackson Arms Catalog No. 14 Supplement — Dallas, Texas.

R. B. Morris — Maryland State Police.

The Gun Report — July, 1958 — Jan., 1961 — July, 1961.

R. W. Wagner, Historian, Colt Firearms Division, Hartford, Connecticut.

Albert W. Lindert, Homewood, Illinois.

Tommy Bish — Piunete, California.

"101 Ranch" *by Collings & England.*

"Historical Hartford Hardware" *by Wm. W. Dalrymple.*

"The Book of Colt Firearms" *by Robt. Q. Suderland & R. L. Wilson.*

"A Study of The Colt Single Action Army Revolver" *by Kopec, Graham, Moore.*

"Saga of The Colt Six-Shooter" *by George E. Virgines.*

"Famous Guns and Gunners" *by George E. Virgines.*

"Colt Commemorative Firearms" *by R. L. Wilson.*

CHAPTER XIII

BIRTH OF A COLT COMMEMORATIVE LEGEND

Have you ever wondered how a commemorative gun is conceived? What research and planning goes into the concept? How much time lapses from the birth of a mere idea to the final product and its presentation to the public? How are the many trials and tribulations that are encountered in such a project finally resolved?

Since 1961 many gun manufacturers have discovered the wide appeal and interest that has been created by commemorative firearms that have flooded the market. This interest has opened a whole new field of collecting for gun enthusiasts, for these replicas duplicate the weapons of the past.

Such gun companies as Colt, Winchester, High Standard, Smith & Wesson, Ruger, Harrington & Richardson, Remington, have gotten on the bandwagon to produce and promote this new type commemorative firearm. The Colt Firearms Company of Hartford, Connecticut, has perhaps been the first and leading producer of these new type commemorative weapons. Colt got into the business of producing these new and unique pieces quite by chance in 1961 when it accepted an order for a contract of a limited number of special marked .22 caliber, single shot Derringers to celebrated the 125th anniversary of the town of Geneseo, Illinois. That same year, Colt celebrated its own 125th anniversary by issuing a special Colt Single Action Army revolver in .45 caliber, beautifully finished and cased.

Since the first commemorative of 1961 was issued by Colt, they have issued more than 130 different commemoratives by 1980. "Birth of a Colt Commemorative Legend" is a story of just how a commemorative is conceived. But first the new golden rule for collectors of "commemorative" guns is "Warning, Do Not Shoot This Gun" and the reason for this strange message for a weapon is as follows: In order to keep these prized pieces in mint condition and assure their future increase in value is to handle them as little as possible, in fact not at all if possible. Commemorative gun collectors strive to keep their prizes in absolute mint condition.

To illustrate exactly what transpires between the mere suggestion of an idea to its final completion, the Arizona Ranger Colt Commemorative was chosen.

It was early in 1968 that the suggestion was submitted to the Colt Firearms Company to produce a gun to honor the Arizona Rangers, and they acknowledged that it would be given serious consideration. Later in the same year, the Colt's Commemorative Advisory Committee announced the acceptance of the proposal for the Arizona Ranger as a subject for a future commemorative. This committee is a group whose membership consists of representatives from dealers, collectors and the Colt Company. Their main purpose is to protect the commemorative collector and to assure that only the most significant events, both historical and national, will be commemorated in distinguished choice. They meet at least twice a year for the purpose of discussing future commemoratives.

Unlike most commemoratives produced, it took almost seven years for the Arizona Ranger piece to become a reality. The selection of Arizona Rangers as a preference for the subject of a commemorative was a natural. They qualified in the category of being a historical group and their background was a most colorful and exciting era of our Western frontier. They typified an appeal that arms collectors would appreciate. Another contributing factor was that the Ranger organization is an active group, which made them a contemporary asset to the project.

The next priority was to find out how receptive Colt was and a series of contacts was made with Sgt. H. S. Copeland of the Arizona Rangers who had the authorization to either approve or reject any proposals and then to forward his suggestions to Colt. It might be mentioned that the name "Arizona Rangers" is copyrighted and so permission had to be granted to use the name on any product.

Colt was most receptive to the proposition but naturally could not react immediately due to other commitments of accepted models in the process of being produced and already other commemoratives being considered. So although the Ranger commemorative was seriously being contemplated, a necessary period of time elapsed before being fully accepted.

Then, in January of 1972, four years later, the good news was received, Colt had accepted the proposed Ranger commemorative.

By February of 1972, Don Mitchell, the then manager of Colt's product marketing, had made plans for producing the new Ranger gun. In part, it was as follows: A Colt "Peacemaker" model, caliber .22 with a 7½-inch barrel, black rubber eagle type grips and gold plated backstrap, trigger guard, trigger and hammer. There would be 26 special guns inscribed with a name of each of the original 26 Rangers on the backstrap and engraved in Colt's "C" style grade. The 26th gun would have the name of the Captain on the backstrap, and a special, deluxe style engraving.

Although this all sounded most appealing, it was not

advisable. When the Rangers were originated in 1901, they were allowed only 14 men. It wasn't until 1903 that they were allowed to increase their strength to 26. At no one time did they have a full force because their roster fluctuated so much for one reason or another. Hence, it would be difficult to determine who were the original 26 Rangers. But unfortunately, before this information was received by Don Mitchell, some advance publicity about the new Ranger Colts, later rescinded, had been released.

To facilitate more definite plans on the final outcome of the Ranger guns, a meeting was arranged in Tucson between Don Mitchell and Sgt. Copeland. The Rangers had favored a Colt Single Action .45 as a commemorative, but Colt had to decline this proposal because of other commitments; and, this would also have pushed the project of the Ranger piece too far into the future. A happy medium was finally agreed upon in which the new "Peacemaker" series with a 5½-inch barrel and other surface changes was to be the new Arizona Ranger commemorative.

Now, finally, both parties concerned were satisfied and it was decided that instead of 2000 units being produced the number would be upped to 3,001 guns and distribution scheduled for the fall of 1972. It wasn't until February, 1973, that Colt had produced 1,600 guns of the intended 3,001, only to encounter a new setback. The Colt factory was shut down because of a strike that was to last for almost six months. This set all production off schedule. To be fair with their customers, Colt initiated a policy of not releasing any of the first 1,600 Ranger units until complete production of the original amount was completed; in this way, all of their customers could obtain this commemorative at the same time. So it wasn't until March of 1974 that the Arizona Ranger Colt began to appear on the market and finally became a reality. It was, perhaps, one of the longest delayed commemoratives ever produced and especially so for the arms enthusiast who anxiously awaits each new model to add to his collection.

It was a most welcome addition to the family of commemoratives and one well worth waiting for. It had run the gamut of changes and setbacks. And, here at last, were the

This Arizona Ranger star was completely custom made by A. A. White in solid silver. It is inscribed on the back, "Engraved by A. A. White for George E. Virgines and AR Colt Comm. SN. 33 AR - 1975".

This is the inscribed silver presentation plaque included with the Arizona Ranger commemorative Colt given to author George E. Virgines by the Colt Firearms Co.

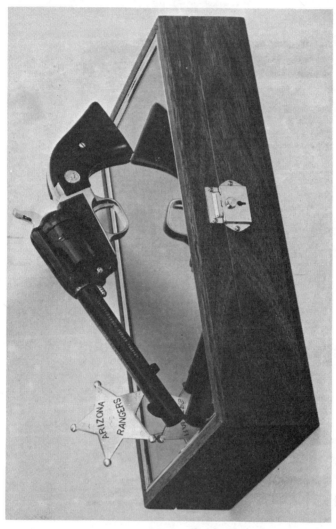

The Colt Arizona Ranger commemorative weapon, caliber .22 rimfire, single action. The case is walnut with a glass top and with it is shown a replica of an Arizona Ranger badge.

final results. The following is a description of this fine new model: Called the "Peacemaker .22", it is the same size as the old Scout models upon which many of the past commemoratives were based. But the new model is totally unique in every way, officially known at the factory as the Model "G". The frame is all steel with the famous Colt color case hardening, barrel and cylinder having the high lustre royal blue finish. The gun also has the original type cylinder spring latch/cylinder pin release, not the old screw-in-the-frame type. The frame itself is marked with the traditional patent dates — "Pat. Sept. 19, 1871 - July 2,72 - Jan. 19,75" — and the famed Rampant Colt. Top of the barrel is marked "Colt's PT. F.A.MFG. Co. Hartford, CT.U.S.A." Left side of the barrel is marked "Arizona Ranger Commemorative". The cylinder is marked three places around, ".22 L.R." To further enhance the Ranger Colt, it is trimmed with a nickel plated backstrap, trigger guard, trigger, hammer and cylinder pin.

An added touch is a finely engraved butt and laminated rosewood grips with a nickel plated Rampant Colt medallion on both sides. The Arizona Rangers had originally suggested a miniature Ranger badge for the grips. To set off this fine piece, it is enclosed in an oiled walnut case with a French-fitted inside bottom lining of deep maroon velvet and a glass, metal-framed cover. Two accessories accompany the gun: One, an exact duplicate of the Arizona Ranger badge in size and engraving which is permanently affixed to the inside of the case; and a booklet on the history of the Arizona Rangers which lends appeal to a most complete package.

It is necessary that the whole package be attractive and have appeal, such as finishes, accessories and casing and that the subject commemorated be of interest both to the old and new commemorative collector. Even the accessories — especially the interesting illustrated and well researched booklets — have become collectors items. As of this date, 14 booklets have accompanied some of the various commemorative models. Although the booklets and other accessories cannot be bought separately, many of these booklets have been noted listed in book catalogs at extraordinary prices, testifying to the desirability they have achieved.

Variations and statistics are always of interest to collectors and the Arizona Ranger Colt is no exception. It is the first Colt Commemorative (.22 caliber) to be issued with a 5½-inch barrel, only the second issued model to be accompanied by a badge in the casing and the second model to be chosen in the Model "G", "Peacemaker" series. Serial numbers range from O-AR to 3000-AR. Serial No. O-AR is reserved for the Colt Company collection.

The final phase of a new model commemorative is its introduction to the public. New commemoratives are announced generally at the NSGA (National Sporting Goods Association) convention show, traditionally held in late January or early February of each year. New commemoratives are also announced through special mail to members of the Colt's Commemorative Collectors Association of America, as well as through regular advertising and publicity channels. The gun is made available through all Colt dealers on a national basis.

What has now become a tradition with the Colt Company is the presentation of new model commemoratives to certain prominent dignitaries, thus completing the circle of birth to distribution. The first presentation Arizona Ranger Commemorative was made in March of 1974 to Governor Jack Williams, which is traditionally serial number "1". Besides the presentation to the governor of Arizona, a second presentation was made to ex-governor of South Dakota, Joe Foss, serial number 1901-AR. Senator Barry Goldwater of Arizona was presented with Serial Number 1G-AR.

Inasmuch as the Colt Firearms Company was moved to produce a commemorative gun honoring the Arizona Rangers, Alvin A. White., the foremost arms engraver and distinguished craftsman, was inspired to create a most unique Arizona Ranger badge. Mr. White is noted for the many finely executed presentation guns he engraved for presidents, VIPs, and other celebrities.

The idea for this dazzling star was conceived by R. L. Wilson, vice president of the A. A. White Engravers, Inc., Manchester, Connecticut; and George E. Virgines, to replace the somewhat plain star that was originally packaged with the

164

Arizona Ranger Colt Commemorative. Using a photograph of an original Arizona Ranger badge for the pattern, Al White very artistically engraved this ranger piece by enhancing it with scrolls and in the center carved of solid silver the rampant colt, trademark of the Colt Company.

This fine representative piece of Alvin A. White's talents completes the circuit of a "Birth of a Commemorative."

BIBLIOGRAPHY

"The Book of Colt Firearms" *by Robt. Q. Sutherland & R. L. Wilson.*

"Colt Commemorative Firearms" *by R. L. Wilson.*

"Saga of The Colt Six-Shooter" *by George E. Virgines.*

"The Arizona Rangers" *by George E. Virgines.*

The Commemorative Collector — Fall — Winter, 1972.

Don Mitchell — Colt Firearms Division — Hartford, Connecticut.

John B. G. Fiedler — Colt Firearms Division — Hartford, Connecticut.

Sgt. Stu Copeland, Historian, Arizona Rangers, Tucson, Arizona.

R. L. Wilson, Manager, A. A. White Engravers, Inc., Manchester, Connecticut

166

CHAPTER XIV

THE LAST LEGEND

On December 19, 1980, the Colt Firearms Company, an old reliable and historic firearms manufacturer, released an ominous and historical news bulletin that startled gun fraternity enthusiasts. The letter is as follows:

"Hartford, CT. December 19, 1980 — Colt Firearms has announced to its distributors that production of Colt Single Action Armies will be discontinued on or about December, 1981. This decision has been made due to current market and economic conditions. Continuous production is scheduled through 1981, however, the phase-out will occur model by model each month. Some models have already been discontinued and this will continue through 1981.

We have no anticipated plans to reintroduce the line.
However, if economic and market conditions warrant, considera-
tion for reintroduction could not occur until 1983 at the earliest. If
the line is reintroduced at a later date, there will be significant
changes in features and characteristics of the guns."

To say the very least this was most disturbing news to
both shooters and collectors about the demise of this famed
and classic revolver that earned the reputation as the "gun
that won the West." It not only helped tame the wild West
frontier, but it was the favorite handgun of cinema and
television cowboy stars for decades. It was the type of gun that
was synonymous with anything and anybody that had to do
with our Western frontier heritage. Its official name was the
Model P, it was called the Colt Single Action Army revolver
in the catalogs, and most affectionately called by a variety of
nick-names such as "Peacemaker", "Six-Shooter", "Frontier
Sixshooter", "Colt .45", "Hog-leg", "Plow-handle", and
many more. To explain and detail all the many variations and
history of this gun has already taken more than a dozen fine
books, and there will probably be more. There is just no last
word for this favorite old "Shootin' Iron".

To pick out one particular Colt Single Action, of all the
various models that were available of this famed gun, as a
favorite for whatever personal reason, could be difficult. This
Colt was just a very unique and representative piece of an era
long gone but not forgotten.

This story deals with the "new" Colt Sheriff's model
.44-40. It is a re-issue of the rare "Sheriff's Model" version of
the classic Single Action Army.

The Sheriff's Model sometimes known as "The World's
Biggest Pocket Pistol" is the ever popular short barrel, ejectorless model that has a heritage going back as far as the 1870's
and 1880's. These short barrel Colts continue to provide all
the unique variations to satisfy every Colt Single Action
collector's whim and fancy. Even the nick-names attached to
this Colt constitute a variety, such as custom model, Store-
keeper and/or Sheriff's Model, hide-a-way-gun, snubbie,

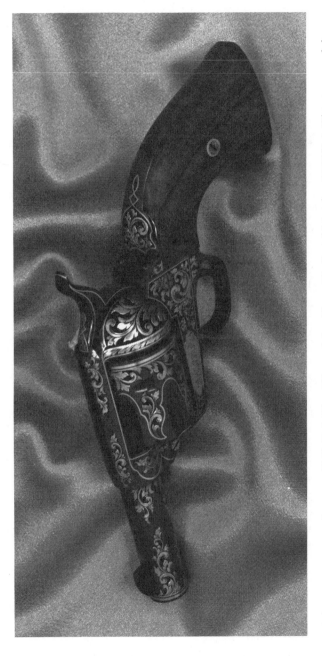

A most unique and ornate 1960 Colt Sheriff's model caliber .45, Serial Number 0263SM. This is one of the finest non-factory engraved Sheriff's model to have been decorated by the master engraver, Lynton McKenzie in 1980.

Steve Englert

The original type of carton and shipping box for the Colt Sheriff's model .44-40, Serial No. SA 42043, as was used by the Colt company in 1981.

The author's choice. One of the last legendary Colts to have been produced in 1981. This is a Colt Sheriff's model .44-40, Serial No. SA 42043, with 3-inch barrel and black eagle grips.

The most publicized advertisement issued by Colt Firearms Co. announced one of the last legendary Colt Sheriff's model .44-40 single actions. At left is the nickle plated model. The other gun is the standard blue case hardened model. The unique badge belongs to the author. This ad appeared in almost every major firearm publication across the United States.

Colt Firearms Division

pocket pistol, pocket peacemaker, and even commemorative because of its limited production. This newest addition to the Colt family will certainly not lack in any way for uniqueness or variety. Even in the 1870's and early 1880's there is evidence that these ejectorless models were supplied on special order basis long before they were listed in Colt's catalogs. In over a century this practice has not changed.

Eliminating the ejector rod assembly from alongside the barrel, which was for ejecting cartridges from the cylinder, and by installing a shorter barrel gave these Sheriff models that extra appeal. The cylinder pin was used to eject the shells. Through the years the barrel lengths of just the ejectorless models have been optional, from 2½ to 7½ inches. Factory engraved Sheriff's models are scarce, to say the least. According to Colt's records only a total of 40 were embellished by the engraver's art.

All Colt Single Action Army revolvers were discontinued in 1940 and then production was resumed once again in 1955 by popular demand of shooters and collectors.

In 1960 a new Colt Sheriff's model was reintroduced in .45 caliber with a 3 inch barrel. Production was limited to only 503 pieces, 25 of these were nickel plated, the balance blued with case hardened frames, and equipped with two piece wood grips. The 1960 Colt Sheriff's Model had a separate serial number range from 0001 SM to 0503 SM. Only two of these 1960 models were factory engraved and on the butts only. However some of the 1960 models were non-factory cased that have become collector's items and also have been engraved by other than factory engravers. One very fine, desirable rarity, and non-factory engraved Sheriff's Model is a 1960 model with Serial Number 0263 SM that was decorated and embellished by the noted gun engraver artist Lynton McKenzie, in 1980. In part this unique piece was described in part as follows: "The engraved detail is finished in a soft "French Gray" to contrast with the rich satin blue and gold." A truely engraver's work of art. It was cased with full accessories by Norbert Ertel.

Once again, in 1980, the "New" Colt Sheriff's Model

.44-40 was presented to the public in a limited number of just slightly more than 3,000 units. To initiate the appeal for this new .44-40 Sheriff's model are the many variations it has to offer. Four different limited model variations were made available. First is Model P1932, Sheriff's model, Standard, quantity: 1000, caliber .44-40, 3 inch barrel, blued with case hardened frame, standard SSA composite stocks with rampant colt and eagle, 1980 retail price $399.95. Second model P1934 is Sheriff's model with dual cylinder and presentation walnut, glass cover case. Quantity: 1,150, caliber .44⁄40, .44 Special, 3 inch barrel, royal blue with case hardened frame. Grips are standard two-piece wood grips without the rampant colt medallion; 1980 retail price $680.95. Third model P1933, quantity: 600, caliber .44-40 and .44 Special, is similar to Model P1934 except it comes in all nickel plate and similar French walnut presentation case; 1980 retail price $680.95. A fourth variation was offered on a price on request basis and that is a factory engraved Sheriff's model, .44-40 and .44 Special, 3-inch barrel, cased with extra cylinder and gold inlaid to customer's specifications. The P1934 and P1933 both are supplied with an extra .44 Special cylinder. Both the royal blued and nickel plated models are marked on the left side of the barrel "Colt Sheriff's Model" as is the Standard model. The two cased models are distinguished by the markings on the right side of the barrel "Colt SAA.44CAL." While the Standard model is marked on the right side of the barrel "Colt SAA.44-40." Also all models are numbered in the standard Colt Single Action Army serial number range. These new models have the "SA" prefix with the serial number which began sometime in 1978 with the Colt Single Action Army serial numbers as opposed to the "SA" suffix marked with the serial numbers, previously.

A new variation is beginning to appear with these new Sheriff models regarding their barrel markings to which the buyer should be alerted. Barrels have been noted with the marking "Colt SAA.44 CAL." that should be on the P1934 Royal Blue are found on the Standard model; and the marking "Colt SAA.44-40." which should be on the P1932 model have been noted on the Royal Blue piece.

174

A question has arisen concerning these snub-nose pistols. Should they be fired and used as a shooter or should they be preserved as collector's items? Many writers of various gun publications have test fired these short barrel Colts and have reported on the whole that they were excellent shooters. While collectors of commemoratives and limited edition guns are observing a new golden rule concerning firearms, "Warning: Do Not Shoot This Gun." If possible in order to keep these very "Special" firearms in mint condition, handling is kept to a bare minimum, thus assuring future increases in value. This new abbreviated barrel piece should fit into this category very appealingly. However, the bottom line is that it is the owner's choice or option.

Perhaps the following might be of interest in relation to this latest Colt Sheriff's model. Noted in all of the advertising pertaining to this new model is a "Deputy United States Marshal" badge which somehow does not relate to a gun marked "Sheriff's Model". The reason for the use of this badge is that it was borrowed from George E. Virgines by Colt in 1979 when the Colt company was seriously contemplating a new Sheriff's model that was going to be known as the "U.S. Marshal" Commemorative, and be so marked. As a commemorative this would have been a most unique piece but according to Colt has been shelved for the time being.

With the phophetic news facing the Colt Single Action Army collector this latest and possibly last, exclusive Sheriff's model should definitely become a classic in its own time.

BIBLIOGRAPHY

Colt Firearms Division, Hartford, Connecticut.
Lyle Grutzmacher, Elk Grove, Illinois.
Steve Englert, Loveland, Colorado.